# BARRON'S BOOK NOTES

## CHARLES DICKENS'S

# *David Copperfield*

BY

Holly Hughes

SERIES COORDINATOR

**Murray Bromberg**
Principal, Wang High School of Queens
Holliswood, New York

**BARRON'S**

BARRON'S EDUCATIONAL SERIES, INC.
Woodbury, New York • London • Toronto • Sydney

## ACKNOWLEDGMENTS

Our thanks to Milton Katz and Julius Liebb for their contribution to the Book Notes series.

*All inquiries should be addressed to:*
Barron's Educational Series, Inc.
113 Crossways Park Drive
Woodbury, New York 11797

*Library of Congress Catalog Card No. 85-4073*

International Standard Book No. 0-8120-3509-7

**Library of Congress Cataloging in Publication Data**

Hughes, Holly.
    Charles Dickens's David Copperfield.

    (Barron's book notes)
    Bibliography: p.134
    Summary: A guide to reading "David Copperfield" with a
critical and appreciative mind encouraging analysis of
plot, style, form, and structure. Also includes
background on the author's life and times, sample
tests, term paper suggestions, and a reading list.
    1. Dickens, Charles, 1812–1870. David Copperfield.
[1. Dickens, Charles, 1812–1870. David Copperfield.
2. English literature—History and criticism] I. Title.
II. Series.
PR4558.H8    1985        823'.8        85-4073
ISBN 0-8120-3509-7

PRINTED IN THE UNITED STATES OF AMERICA

567        550        987654321

# CONTENTS

| | |
|---|---|
| Advisory Board | iv |
| How to Use This Book | v |
| **THE AUTHOR AND HIS TIMES** | 1 |
| **THE NOVEL** | 8 |
| The Plot | 8 |
| The Characters | 12 |
| Other Elements | 28 |
|     Setting | 28 |
|     Themes | 29 |
|     Style | 32 |
|     Point of View | 33 |
|     Form and Structure | 34 |
| **The Story** | 35 |
| **A STEP BEYOND** | 124 |
| Tests and Answers | 124 |
| Term Paper Ideas and other Topics for Writing | 132 |
| Further Reading | 134 |
|     Critical Works | 134 |
|     Author's Other Works | 135 |
| Glossary | 136 |
| The Critics | 137 |

# ADVISORY BOARD

# HOW TO USE THIS BOOK

You have to know how to approach literature in order to get the most out of it. This *Barron's Book Notes* volume follows a plan based on methods used by some of the best students to read a work of literature.

Begin with the guide's section on the author's life and times. As you read, try to form a clear picture of the author's personality, circumstances, and motives for writing the work. This background usually will make it easier for you to hear the author's tone of voice, and follow where the author is heading.

Then go over the rest of the introductory material—such sections as those on the plot, characters, setting, themes, and style of the work. Underline, or write down in your notebook, particular things to watch for, such as contrasts between characters and repeated literary devices. At this point, you may want to develop a system of symbols to use in marking your text as you read. (Of course, you should only mark up a book you own, not one that belongs to another person or a school.) Perhaps you will want to use a different letter for each character's name, a different number for each major theme of the book, a different color for each important symbol or literary device. Be prepared to mark up the pages of your book as you read. Put your marks in the margins so you can find them again easily.

Now comes the moment you've been waiting for—the time to start reading the work of literature. You may want to put aside your *Barron's Book Notes* volume until you've read the work all the way through. Or you may want to alternate, reading the *Book Notes* analysis of each section as soon as you have finished reading the corresponding part of the original. Before you move on, reread crucial passages you don't fully understand. (Don't take this guide's analysis for granted—make up your own mind as to what the work means.)

Once you've finished the whole work of literature, you may want to review it right away, so you can firm up your ideas about what it means. You may want to leaf through the book concentrating on passages you marked in reference to one character or one theme. This is also a good time to reread the *Book Notes* introductory material, which pulls together insights on specific topics.

When it comes time to prepare for a test or to write a paper, you'll already have formed ideas about the work. You'll be able to go back through it, refreshing your memory as to the author's exact words and perspective, so that you can support your opinions with evidence drawn straight from the work. Patterns will emerge, and ideas will fall into place; your essay question or term paper will almost write itself. Give yourself a dry run with one of the sample tests in the guide. These tests present both multiple-choice and essay questions. An accompanying section gives answers to the multiple-choice questions as well as suggestions for writing the essays. If you have to select a term paper topic, you may choose one from the list of suggestions in this book. This guide also provides you with a reading list, to help you when you start research for a term paper, and a selection of provocative comments by critics, to spark your thinking before you write.

# THE AUTHOR AND HIS TIMES

"I seem to be sending some part of myself into the Shadowy World," Charles Dickens wrote in a letter just before he finished the final chapter of *David Copperfield*. Dickens, as a matter of course, became intensely involved with all his books while he was writing them. His daughter once recalled how her father would sit in his study, speaking the characters' speeches as he wrote them, making faces, giggling, or sighing with emotion. But in 1869, the year before he died, Dickens wrote that *Copperfield* was still his "favourite child." Why was he so attached to this novel, of all the masterpieces he had created?

Readers of his own time assumed, of course, that *David Copperfield* was thinly disguised autobiography. After all, it was the first novel Dickens had written in the first person. Like Dickens, David is a novelist who started out as a political reporter. David's initials are even Dickens' in reverse (though Dickens himself was surprised when that coincidence was pointed out to him). But now that more is known about Dickens' life, it is clear that he changed the facts a great deal to write *David Copperfield*. Let's compare the two stories.

Whereas David is a naive village boy and an orphan, Charles Dickens spent his childhood in the bustling seaside towns of Portsmouth and Chatham, on the southern coast of England, and was the second of eight children. His parents, John and

Elizabeth Dickens, were charming and utterly irresponsible people, who lived far beyond Mr.
Dickens' salary as a civil servant. When their financial situation grew desperate, they packed up
and moved to London, to a cramped, grubby house,
where bill-collectors were continually hammering
at the door. Finally John Dickens was arrested for
debt and sent to Marshalsea Prison. Most of the
family moved in with him (a typical arrangement
in debtors' prison, which was a fairly open place),
but twelve-year-old Charles lived outside in rented
rooms so he could work in a factory, pasting labels
on bottles of bootblacking (a kind of shoe polish).

Although this experience lasted only four months,
it scarred Charles so profoundly that he never spoke
of it to anyone. We only know about it from a
fragment of writing he once silently showed to his
closest friend—and from his fictional treatment of
it, when he sends David Copperfield to work in a
similar sweatshop. Dickens never really forgave his
parents—especially his mother, who'd pushed the
idea hardest—for sending him to the factory. Perhaps that is why he later identified so readily with
the orphans in his novels, and wrote glowing descriptions of the "perfect" family he felt he'd never
had. It's interesting, however, that John and Elizabeth Dickens' delightful personalities seem to have
been the models for David's friends, the Micawbers, while Dickens created for David a wicked
stepfather, Mr. Murdstone—a worthy target for the
anger that still boiled deep in Dickens' heart.

A surprise inheritance from a distant relative freed
the Dickens family from prison. Yet it took a bit of
arguing for Charles to persuade his mother to let
him quit working and go back to school. Unfor-

tunately, the school he was finally sent to, Wellington House, was run by a cruel headmaster who liked to beat boys—much like Mr. Creakle at Salem House, where David begins school. Whereas David later gets a good education from Dr. Strong, Charles had to make do with the little he learned at Wellington House. Again Charles was resentful, sensing that he had talent and feeling thwarted by his inferior education. He went to work first as a clerk in a lawyer's office and then, dissatisfied with law, learned shorthand so that he could get a job taking down the debates in Parliament for a newspaper that published transcripts of them. David Copperfield does this, too.

When he was seventeen, Dickens fell in love with Maria Beadnell, who by all accounts was as winsome and flirtatious as David Copperfield's sweetheart, Dora. Maria's father, a banker, apparently disapproved of Dickens, and after a couple of years, he sent his daughter abroad to separate them, just as Dora's father threatens to do in *David Copperfield*. Maria showed no interest in Charles after her return, and he felt crushed. In describing David Copperfield's courtship of Dora, Dickens may have been reliving his infatuation with Maria—and, in David's marriage to Dora, Dickens may have been speculating on what could have happened if he had married Maria. (Soon after publishing *David Copperfield*, Dickens would run into Maria Beadnell again and discover, with chagrin, that the living model for Dora had become a fat and extremely silly middle-aged matron.)

Hurt by Maria's rejection, Dickens threw himself into hard work. Then began another courtship, this time with Catherine Hogarth, the daughter of a fellow journalist. He was so desperate to settle down that he didn't judge his prospective bride carefully, for they were not really suited for each other in the long run. David's disappointment with his "child-wife" Dora may be realistically drawn from Charles' eventual discontent with the woman he did marry—dull, sweet Catherine.

But before he could get married, Dickens, like David, had to work furiously to set himself up in his career. He had won some fame as a journalist, and in 1836, just before his wedding, he published his first work of fiction—*Pickwick Papers*, a loosely connected series of comical sketches. This book appeared in serial installments, as all of his novels would. Month by month Dickens' fame mushroomed. Suddenly he was a celebrity. Even while *Pickwick* was still appearing, Dickens began a new book, *Oliver Twist*, which also was a best-seller— and he kept producing hits, year after year. By the time *David Copperfield*, his seventh novel, appeared in 1850, Charles Dickens was a British national institution.

To be a best-selling novelist in nineteenth-century England was practically like being a pop star today. In those days before movies, radio, or television, people read novels as their main form of entertainment. They didn't think of them as "literature." Dickens' books did a lot to make novels more respectable, because his novels were read by all levels of society. Intellectuals pored over them for their political satire and social commentary. Middle-class families in their cozy parlors looked forward to reading Dickens' latest book, admiring his sentimental scenes and moral messages. In poorer neighborhoods, people might gather in groups, breathlessly listening to it being read aloud; they laughed at the broad comedy and gasped at the thrilling suspense. Dickens had hit upon a formula for pleasing everybody: he spanned all levels of society with his multilayered plots and huge cast of characters, and he ended each serial installment with a thrilling climax, to make his readers rush out to buy the next month's.

Having begun his career as a political journalist, Dickens used his novels to examine problems he saw in society. In *Oliver Twist*, for example, he exposed the wretched living conditions of England's poorhouses and slums. In *Nicholas Nickleby* he attacked the cruel, negligent Yorkshire boarding schools. In *Bleak House* he went after the Court of Chancery. Thus, in *David Copperfield*, he protests against the sexual mores of his age that condemned "fallen" women—unmarried women (usually poor) who had affairs or gave birth to illegitimate children. He also shows the misery of child labor. (While his original readers probably assumed the warehouse scenes were invented for purposes of satire, we now know that Dickens was recording actual memories of his secret past.) Dickens criticizes the antiquated legal institution of Doctors' Commons in a few passages. He also devotes a chapter to satirizing prison reform.

Some of these bursts of satire are not really central to the book. It's almost as if Dickens felt he had to include satire, because that was what he was known for. Much of Dickens' popularity was based on his reputation as a social critic. Many middle-class Victorians liked to think of themselves as concerned citizens, whose rational, humane efforts were creating the perfect society.

Dickens was, like them, a reformer but not a radical. Some of the conditions he criticized had already been improved by these reformers by the time he wrote about them. Dickens had no interest in tearing apart the framework of society—only in improving it to come closer to his ideals of justice and Christian charity. He was actually more of a conservative than many readers realize.

Some readers see the publication of *David Copperfield* as the turning point in Dickens' career. Until then, in novels such as *Oliver Twist*, *Nicholas Nickleby*, and *Dombey and Son*, he had written very much with his audience in mind. All the elements of comedy, melodrama, mystery, and social criticism appear in those books, for the author seems most concerned with entertaining his readers. But *David Copperfield* gave Dickens an opportunity to be more personal, to write about his own life and explore individual human nature rather than society as a whole. His later novels, such as *Little Dorrit*, *Great Expectations*, and *Our Mutual Friend*, move further into this psychological territory and leave satire further behind.

At the time he wrote *David Copperfield*, Dickens was popular, admired, famous, and rich, just as David Copperfield is at the end of the novel. Yet Dickens' later years did not bring him the happy ending he had written for David. He found that the success he had driven so hard for only increased the demands upon his time and energies. He felt his ideal of domestic harmony falling to pieces. In 1858 he and his wife separated—a scandalous action in those days. Though his ten children remained with him in his huge country house, he was bitterly disappointed by his sons' failures.

Melancholy, restless, and irritable, he continued to write novels, but they became tinged with pessimism about human nature and society. He tried to stave off depression with more and more work, as well as with amateur theatricals, lecture tours, and dramatic readings from his own works. But this frenzied activity only hastened his death of a stroke in 1870.

Like most great artists, Dickens was a complex man, perhaps more complex than his character David Copperfield. His writer's instincts compelled him to shape the events of his life into a richer, more artistic form when he wrote about them in *David Copperfield*. If you want to read a biography of Dickens, there are plenty to choose from. But if you want to read a great work of literature, turn to *David Copperfield*.

# THE NOVEL

## The Plot

The day David Copperfield is born, his rich, eccentric Aunt Betsey Trotwood storms away in disapproval because the new baby is not a girl. David is raised by his pretty young mother, widowed before he was born, and their loyal servant, Clara Peggotty. But this idyllic childhood is interrupted when black-whiskered Mr. Murdstone begins to court Mrs. Copperfield. David happily goes with Peggotty to visit her family in Yarmouth—her fisherman brother, Daniel, and his adopted nephew and niece, Ham and Little Em'ly. When David returns home, however, Murdstone and David's mother have married, and not long after, Murdstone's sister Jane moves in. The Murdstones intimidate David's mother and terrorize David, until one day he bites Mr. Murdstone's hand in a rebellious rage. As punishment, David is sent to Salem House, a boarding school near London, where he is miserable. However, he does make two friends—dull, decent Tommy Traddles, and brilliant James Steerforth, an older student whom David idolizes.

David's schooldays are interrupted by the news that his mother and her new baby have died. After their funeral, David is not sent back to Salem House but kept idle at home. Peggotty is fired and marries the local wagon-driver, Barkis. Eventually Murdstone announces that he has provided for David by getting him a job, working in the London warehouse of Murdstone's wine business. David, who is only ten, begins to work several hours a day, six days a week, alongside grimy, uneducated boys, for only a few shillings. The only light in this grim period is his friendship with the debt-ridden Micawber family, who rent a bedroom in their apartment to David. When the Micawbers leave London, David decides to run away to his Aunt Betsey, whom he has never met. On foot, penniless, beset by thieves and con men, David makes the journey to Aunt Betsey's cottage in Dover.

Though disconcerted by this ragged child on her doorstep, Betsey soon warms to him, especially after the Murdstones come to collect him and she sees what his alternative is. David settles happily into a new circle of friends: simpleminded Mr. Dick, who lives at Betsey's; Betsey's lawyer Mr. Wickfield, his sweet daughter Agnes, and his fawning law clerk Uriah Heep; the master of David's new school, Dr. Strong, his young wife Annie, and her flirtatious cousin Jack Maldon.

David grows to young manhood, and, once he has finished school, his aunt sends him to London to choose a career. In London, David runs into his old friend James Steerforth, who takes David home to meet his proud, possessive mother and her companion, the intense Rosa Dartle. In turn, David takes Steerforth with him to Yarmouth, to visit Peggotty and her family. Steerforth is a great hit with everyone, and he buys a boat so he can sail down there regularly.

Back in London, David and Betsey go to the law offices of Spenlow and Jorkins; in Doctors' Commons, where David is taken in as a trainee in the firm. David meets Mr. Spenlow's pretty daughter Dora and falls madly in love. He also meets Tommy

Traddles again, and finds that he is boarding with the Micawbers! Then David is called to Yarmouth for Barkis' funeral. That night, Emily, who has been engaged to Ham, disappears, leaving a note that she has run off with Steerforth—with no plans to be married.

Aunt Betsey arrives in London with the news that she has lost all her money and is moving in to live with David on a tiny income. In spite of this setback, David continues to court Dora secretly until, after Mr. Spenlow's sudden death, they can announce their engagement. But Mr. Spenlow left Dora penniless, and David must work hard to earn enough money to marry. He takes on a second job as secretary to his old schoolmaster, Dr. Strong, who has now moved to London. David also learns shorthand and begins working as a reporter covering parliamentary debates. He finally makes enough money to marry Dora, and they move into a cottage across the street from Aunt Betsey. David discovers that his adorable bride is totally unfit to manage a household, and, though he still loves her, he despairs about their domestic life. He throws himself into his work and begins to win some fame as a fiction writer. At about this time he witnesses a reconciliation between Annie and Dr. Strong, who have been unhappy together because of Jack Maldon's flirtations with Annie. As David hears Annie tell Dr. Strong how his love for her has given her strength and wisdom, David wonders if his own marriage will survive so well.

News from Canterbury, from David's old friends the Wickfields, becomes steadily gloomier. Mr. Wickfield, who is depressed and drinking too much, has had his business virtually taken over by Uriah Heep, who also has hopes of marrying Agnes. The usually unemployed Mr. Micawber now works for Heep, and his personality has become strangely secretive and harsh, to Mrs. Micawber's despair. David and Traddles meet Micawber in London, and learn that he, too, is in Heep's power. But he intends, with help, to expose the villain. While Traddles helps Micawber to uncover evidence against Heep, David helps Daniel Peggotty find Emily, who has returned, a ruined woman, to London. She and her uncle make plans to emigrate to Australia, where her past will be unknown.

Meanwhile, after a stillbirth, Dora has fallen gravely ill. David leaves her bedside to go to Canterbury to watch Micawber and Traddles confront Heep with their knowledge of his schemes. Heep is thrown out, Mr. Wickfield's name is cleared, and Betsey's "lost" investments are recovered. Betsey suggests to Micawber that he and his family emigrate to Australia, too, and lends him some money for a fresh start.

Back in London, David nurses Dora, but it is Agnes, sisterly and serene, who is with her when she finally dies. Numb with grief, David helps the emigrants prepare to leave, and agrees to take a letter from Emily to Ham. But a wicked storm hits Yarmouth that night, and David sees Ham, who seems indifferent to life now, swim out to save people from a shipwreck. David alone recognizes the ship's last victim as Steerforth. Ironically, Ham drowns trying to save the man who ruined his happiness. Steerforth's lifeless body is washed up on shore.

The emigrants leave for Australia, and David goes to Switzerland for several months to recover from his grief. Eventually he writes a novel about his experiences. He also thinks a lot about Agnes

Wickfield, realizes that he has always been in love with her, and regrets that she has shown only sisterly feelings toward him. Returning to England, he finally confesses his feelings to Agnes and learns that she has always loved him, too. They marry, have children, and live happily ever after.

# The Characters

## David Copperfield

Because David Copperfield is the narrator, many readers have assumed he is a self-portrait of Dickens. There are several similar incidents in their lives (see "The Author And His Times"), but how similar are their personalities?

Some readers believe that David is simply a portrait of a typical young gentleman of the early Victorian age. He has a middle-class gentleman's education (a good secondary school but no university degree). He holds some liberal beliefs; for example, he criticizes Doctors' Commons and the parliamentary debates. But on the whole he is a supporter of the Establishment. He doesn't question the social conventions that judge his friend Emily to be "ruined" because she has had an affair. He's convinced that it's important to work hard, succeed in a career, and make money. He believes in God, but only as a vague idea—you never see him going to church as an adult. He places a high value on domestic harmony, and thinks that a woman's place is in the home.

Other readers say David is too good to be true. They think that Dickens was trying to deny his own selfishness and insecurity by showing himself in David as a decent, generous young fellow. They point out that David is much more realistic as a child than as an adult. As a boy, he can't pay attention in church, he resents the Murdstones for coming between him and his mother, and he feels sorry for himself when he is punished. Even as he grieves over his mother's death, he basks in the special attention he's getting. But once David grows up, he becomes a model citizen. He bears the burden of his wife Dora's failures; he remains loyal to his treacherous friend Steerforth; he spends a lot of time and energy helping the Strongs, the Wickfields, the Micawbers, and the Peggottys with their problems. He is terribly modest about his career as a writer. Readers who see David in this light feel that it's fitting that he ends up married to such a noble, sexless creature as Agnes. In a later book, *Great Expectations*, they point out, Dickens finally created an honest picture of himself in the narrator, Pip, who criticizes himself as a snob and an ungrateful profligate.

Other readers say that David does have flaws, many of the same ones Dickens had. David's self-centeredness as a child continues into his adult years. For example, he can't help but think of how his future is changed when his Aunt Betsey loses her money. He's also a terrible judge of people. He is blind to the truth about the women he loves, both Dora and Agnes. He underestimates Mr. Dick, Traddles, and Annie Strong, but on the other hand can never see the weakness in Steerforth. He can be impatient and demanding with Dora, yet he's so shy and insecure that he can't deal with servants or waiters. David sometimes seems obsessed with work, orderliness, and money, and can't always see how dull it makes him.

In the book's opening sentence, David asks you

to decide whether or not he is the hero of his own life—judging from what the book shows you. You can take the word "hero" in several different senses:

1.  The hero is the central character, or protagonist. Of course, since David is the narrator, he appears in nearly every scene of the book. But the novel has several plots. In some of them, David is just an observer of the action.

2.  The hero is the most admirable person in the book. Consider, as you read, whether you think David is admirable. Is he a good person? Is he too good to be believed? Would you want to be like him?

3.  The hero of David's own life is the person who deserves the credit for his success and happiness. As you read, think about how David feels about himself. Do you think he sees himself as the "hero" of his life? Why?

4.  The hero is the focus of the themes of the book. As you read and decide what the main themes are, ask yourself if they all relate to David. Watch, too, how the subplots interconnect. Dickens' themes develop from a pattern of all the plots together, mirroring, shadowing, and reversing each other. Is Dickens developing a view of the world as a whole, or do all these themes lead you back to an understanding of David?

## Aunt Betsey Trotwood
Anyone who says that Dickens can't create believable women characters is overlooking Aunt Betsey. From her first bold, comic entrance in Chapter 1, she is one of the book's strongest characters.

Orphan David instinctively flees to her cottage in Dover in spite of the stories he's heard about her, because he needs a stable home. Beneath her gruff exterior, she's a real softie. She has already taken in Mr. Dick, and soon agrees to take in David, especially after meeting the Murdstones, who arouse her feisty spirits. Aunt Betsey may at first seem like a modern feminist, rebelling against the male-dominated system by approving only of girl babies and by teaching her servant girls to give up men. But she isn't as inflexible as her opinions sound. The servant girls always get married, and Betsey comes to love David as much as she ever could have loved his never-born sister.

Although Betsey begins as a comic character—almost a caricature—she becomes more real as the book goes on. She's not much good as a substitute mother for David. She doesn't have that kind of affectionate nature, and she seems awkward caring for a small boy. But Betsey does become rather like a second father to David. She protects their home fiercely, driving away the trespassing donkeys, and physically shields David from the Murdstones. Though she's comically opinionated and brusque, she's shrewd enough to see the truth about such characters as Mr. Wickfield and Mr. Dick. With businesslike briskness she handles such matters as arranging for David's schooling, changing her will to make him her heir, and paying for his entry into a profession.

Therefore, it's startling when she shows up on David's doorstep in London, announcing that she has handled her finances badly and is virtually broke. This is a signal for a shift in generations: the "son" David must begin to provide for the "father" Betsey. David changes with this new responsibility, but so does Betsey. She seems vulnerable at last. She begins to warm up to Peggotty and even becomes fond of Dora (though she can see that David is "blind" to marry her). When David's marriage falters, Betsey is a great emotional support, advising him to be more patient and gentle with his bride (this from the woman who bullied Clara Copperfield!). A mysterious figure haunting Betsey's doorstep from time to time seems to threaten her. When she finally reveals that he is her former husband and admits how much she still feels for him, it's easier for you to understand why she developed that tough shell in the first place. While other characters have to learn to love more wisely, Betsey has to learn that it's all right to let her heart rule sometimes. This adds a vital dimension to the novel's view of life and love.

## Dora Spenlow

Like many other romantic heroines in Dickens' novels, Dora is tiny, childish, almost doll-like (perhaps Dickens' first love, Maria Beadnell, was like that). Though she's a flirt, she isn't very sexy. David's notions about her are romantic, not physical. After they are married he seems almost amazed to be left alone with her, as though he never imagined going so far as to sleep with her. But remember that it's David who idealizes Dora and describes her like a doll, because Dickens is satirizing a young man's romantic foolishness. If you read beyond what David says about her, however, you can discover a three-dimensional person in Dora. She isn't to blame for her immaturity and ignorance. Her father obviously spoiled and overprotected her, and David falls into the same pattern. She has enough wisdom to know that she has disappointed David, and she understands better than he does that she can only be herself. Although she seems shallow and manipulative during their courtship, with her obnoxious dog Jip and her cliché-ridden friend Julia Mills, her loyalty and affection for David never waiver during their brief marriage.

With her sweet, loving nature, her pretty face, and her gullible naive ways, Dora is very much like David's mother. David adored his mother. Perhaps that's why he falls in love with Dora, and why he can't see her shortcomings. When David tries to "form her mind," he is really doing just what Mr. Murdstone did to Mrs. Copperfield, although in a milder fashion. David is as much to blame as Dora for the failures in their marriage.

## Agnes Wickfield

Dora may be the romantic heroine of the book, but Dickens saw Agnes as "the real heroine." From her first entrance, she is almost encircled by a halo. David envisions her as a stained-glass window or an angelic statue, with her hand pointing up to heaven, but he never really tells us what she looks like. He refers only to her beautiful spirit and her good influence on him, as though she were simply a symbol of his conscience. Dora, with her silly lapdog, always seems like a child, but Agnes is motherly even as a young girl, with her housewifely basket of keys at her waist.

Many readers object to Agnes, saying she is an unreal vision of the pure, good, wise woman Dickens longed for. Dickens' fondness for his wife's sister Mary, who lived with them when they were first married, seems to have had a level of sexual attraction in it, so perhaps when David says he loves Agnes as a "sister," Dickens meant this to be more romantic than it sounds. But to many readers, Agnes doesn't seem human. She's unnaturally selfless, self-contained, and noble. She lets David confide all his teenage crushes to her, and she becomes Dora's best friend, even though she herself has secretly been in love with David all her life. She never responds, even with a shudder, to Uriah Heep's repulsive attentions to her. She seems passionless and imperturbable until the last few chapters, when her feelings for David begin to show through.

Remember that you are seeing Agnes through David's eyes, and he is notoriously blind to other people's true natures. Remember, too, that she's the only child of a melancholy, aging father, and her devotion to him has colored her whole life. Consider the lessons David learned from his first marriage, and then you will be prepared to comment on Agnes's suitability as the heroine of this novel.

## Mr. & Mrs. Micawber

The Micawbers are totally irresponsible and totally loveable. As Mr. Micawber loses job after job, as debts pile up and the family keeps growing, they thrive on cheery, optimistic fantasies. While David is their boarder, Mr. Micawber always addresses him as an equal, and Mrs. Micawber seems surprised to notice he's a child. This shows how factory work has aged David prematurely, but it also emphasizes how childishly impractical the Micawbers are. David's experience of their precarious life-style teaches him to become a practical, hard-working man himself. Nevertheless, their affection, liveliness, and loyalty ("I never will desert Mr. Micawber" is Mrs. Micawber's slogan) give David a model of a truly loving home.

The Micawbers are technically caricatures—exaggerated figures who don't seem capable of psychological growth as more realistic characters do. Mrs. Micawber is always yearning for her parents' home. Mr. Micawber is always writing wordy letters. But one hallmark of Dickens' comic genius is to create caricatures with satisfying, lifelike energy. Listen to Mr. Micawber speak, for example (it's said that Dickens drew this florid, high-flown verbal style from his own father). The long, breathless sentences, the extreme dramatic poses, the stock phrases ("in short," "something will turn up"), the pompous formal language—they're so outrageous, you end up believing he's real.

Because Micawber is such a successful caricature, some readers lose interest in him when he helps expose Uriah Heep, or when he succeeds in Australia, because they feel that his reform isn't believable. Some readers also object to the way the Micawbers coincidentally pop up throughout the novel, in unlikely places. Yet others feel that this is natural, that the Micawbers are so full of life that they can't help bursting into every plot.

## The Murdstones
While the Micawbers are comic caricatures, the Murdstones are caricatures of villains. David resents how they disrupt his happy home, and that distorts his—and therefore your—view of them.

When he first meets Mr. Murdstone, David only notices he has "beautiful black hair," but as soon as David starts to feel jealous, Mr. Murdstone is pictured as a black-hearted demon. By the time Miss Murdstone arrives, David sees them both as ogres. He describes them with a child's stubborn exaggeration, and doesn't try to understand their motives. Whenever they later appear, David automatically despises them.

But who are they underneath? Mr. Murdstone, at least, seems more human than his sister. Although he tortures his gentle wife by teaching her "firmness," the way she clings to him shows that Murdstone has somehow gained her affection. David doesn't show you their private moments together, so you have to imagine that there's another side to Murdstone. David thinks Murdstone makes a career of destroying young widows, but it's clear that the man really grieves when David's mother dies. Does that soften your opinion of Murdstone?

Jane Murdstone is stronger, colder, and more heartless than her brother. Dickens makes her seem inhuman by comparing her to metallic objects, especially locks, chains, and prisons. In a society where a spinster is a dependent creature, she uses her power over her brother to secure a home for herself. Notice how she pretends to defer to him, then continually adds her own vicious comments while he's lecturing his wife or trying to negotiate with Betsey Trotwood. Jane's attachment to her brother is almost unnatural, as though she is secretly, jealously in love with him. The Murdstones are villains, but Dickens is skillful enough to also show you the pain that may lie behind a villain's actions.

## Uriah Heep

Uriah Heep is one of those people who automatically give you the creeps. He's bony and pale, with a slight fuzz of red hair and intense, lashless red-brown eyes. He looks like a skeleton; his hands are cold and clammy. He is intensely physical—always writhing and rubbing himself—and Dickens often compares him to animals. Heep is so physically repulsive that he fascinates David at first, but later it revolts David to think of him even touching Agnes.

When you first meet Uriah, he's only about fifteen, but he's an expert in the art of hypocrisy. As he grows older, he becomes more skillful at his nasty games, slowly taking over Mr. Wickfield's business and then his home. Uriah's trademark is to play himself down, saying how humble he is. He puts other people on the defensive and then trips them up by their own vanity. It's an amazingly effective power play, and that's why it's maddening to watch. Even when David tells him off, Uriah pretends to cringe more "umbly" than ever, so that David's anger suddenly looks stupid and selfish. Uriah plays being a worm for all it's worth.

Dickens establishes Uriah Heep as a caricature, outrageously awful, with his stock phrases and gestures and his weird mother behind him like his double. (They almost seem like aliens from another planet!) But just as you've learned to hate Uriah, in Chapter XXXIX he explains the warped upbringing that made him so hungry for power, money, and revenge. You'll have to consider whether or not this excuses Uriah. Is Uriah evil inside because his repulsive looks made him a social outcast, or is his repulsive appearance a symbol of the evil within him? How do you think you would respond to him?

## James Steerforth

David admires his boyhood idol, James Steerforth, so much that he makes the older boy fairly glow on the page. Steerforth is like the brother David never had. He's handsome, charming, talented, carelessly generous—the complete opposite of the timid or repressed people David's grown up with. And, like Dora, Steerforth shows real affection for David, which means a lot to lonely David. Maybe you've known people like this. Just when you're getting fed up with them, they turn on the charm and you can't help but forgive them. Dickens, however, conveys Steerforth's self-centered shallowness by Steerforth's own speeches, by the reactions of sensible characters like Tommy Traddles and Agnes Wickfield, and by melodramatic scenes at Steerforth's home. Watching Steerforth squander his talent, you can admire David more for making the most of his.

David is able to list his friend's flaws, but they never really sway him from his adoration. Perhaps that's why, in spite of all the hints Dickens drops about what's going to happen to Steerforth and Emily, David is still surprised when they run off together. It's also why he doesn't hate Steerforth for seducing Emily. When all is said, Steerforth is undeniably attractive. It's hard to blame Emily for running off with a lover like that, and you can't blame David for still admiring Steerforth, even as he watches him die in the shipwreck—a fitting symbol for the lives he has wrecked.

# Emily

Dickens' political "cause" in this novel is the plight
of fallen women (he was involved with running a
home for such women in London). Emily is Dickens' main example of a fallen woman, and therefore, to make his social comment, he is very careful
to present her in a sympathetic light. He introduces her as "Little Em'ly," a playful, spirited child,
so your first impression is of her innocence and
freshness. Only later, when David revisits the Peggottys, can you sense the doom hanging over her—
a fatal hunger for adventure, for being "a lady."
Yet Emily is by nature a lady. Even her speech is
aristocratic, unlike the dialect of her Uncle Dan
and cousin Ham. In some ways, Dickens blames
the class system for her fate. Society's double
standard will punish Emily, but not Steerforth, for
their affair.

Emily's character gradually becomes less and less
distinct. Although she was David's childhood
sweetheart, his romantic interest fades after they
grow up. Mr. Omer, the local undertaker, tells
David about her, while Emily herself slides silently
in and out. The anguish of a village girl's shame
is voiced dramatically by Martha Endell, but Emily's shame is told only in her letters. After she
returns to England from her scandalous life on the
Continent, David sees her only through a doorway
and across a crowded ship. Even Ham doesn't talk
with her again, though he has forgiven her for
jilting him. Maybe Dickens doesn't want you to
see a "sinful woman" up close, or maybe he's emphasizing what an outcast she has become. Although Emily's uncle takes her back, most girls in
her position weren't so lucky. Though she makes

a new home in Australia, she chooses to remain cut off from life, unmarried. As a Victorian, Dickens can't approve of her moral lapse—he only asks pity for her.

## Clara Copperfield

Because David idealizes his mother, he describes her as a hazy figure, more important as an emotional source than as a real physical figure. She's pretty, affectionate, and too gentle to protect herself (let alone David) from the Murdstones. David's view is true as far as it goes. Her servant Peggotty and Mr. Murdstone both love her, too, and she responds lovingly to them. From her speeches and actions, however, you can draw some other conclusions about her. She is timid—Aunt Betsey, Jane Murdstone, and even Peggotty dominate her. She's gullible and shallow, willing to adopt the opinions of both her husbands. She's selfish, sometimes quarreling like a spoiled child with Peggotty, and she doesn't seem to consider David's reaction when she decides to marry Edward Murdstone. She's weak and a little foolish, but she does give her son the love he needs, and he never gets over losing her.

## Clara Peggotty

Practical, sturdy, loyal, Clara Peggotty provides whatever motherly qualities Clara Copperfield lacks, and the two halves make a warm, secure whole for young David. Peggotty emerges as a force of love and life in the house in opposition to the Murdstones. When David goes away, first to school and later to work, Peggotty's letters give him a sense of continuity with home. Even after she marries the wagon-driver Barkis, she always keeps a room for David, and she preserves cherished relics of his past, such as the crocodile book and her sewing box. Through Peggotty, David gains respect for honest, working-class values. Her constancy and affection run like a reassuring thread throughout the novel.

## Daniel Peggotty

When David first visits Dan Peggotty's ingenious boat-house, he loves it not only because it's like a little boy's fantasy, but also because it offers something he doesn't have at home: a generous, manly father figure. Dan has taken in Ham, Emily, and the widow Mrs. Gummidge out of sheer big-heartedness—a sharp contrast to Mr. Murdstone's grudging acceptance of David. Though he is rough, modest, and inarticulate, Dan's dignity and generous heart make him a natural gentleman. But after his happy home is destroyed, this humble working-class figure seems to change. Some readers feels that his obsession with finding Emily reveals an almost unhealthy attachment to his niece. Others think that in his search he turns into a mythical figure—the wandering spirit of forgiveness and hope. Perhaps it is fitting that at the end of the novel he should lead a group of emigrants to Australia to start new lives.

## Thomas Traddles

At Mr. Creakle's school, dull, decent Tommy Traddles is a victim not only of Creakle's cruelty but also of Steerforth's careless wit. Young Traddles is a pathetic figure, compulsively doodling skeletons. Yet when David meets him years later in

London, Traddle's steady honesty makes him a standard to compare David to: as a lover (Traddles is comically engaged for years to his Sophy), as a young man trying to get ahead in his career (Traddles helps David appreciate hard work), and as a dependable friend. Though he remains a slightly comic figure, with his hair sticking up ridiculously on end, you can't sell him short. He performs wonders in helping to expose Uriah Heep, and eventually the "second-rate" schoolboy becomes quite a success.

## Mr. Dick

Aunt Betsey's friend Mr. Dick may be simple-minded, but his simple thoughts sometimes go right to the heart of the matter. When he first appears, his obvious statements are comical. Aunt Betsey asks his advice on what to do with David and then treats his feeble replies as pearls of wisdom. Later in the book, however, Mr. Dick really does act with a wisdom of the heart in bringing the Strongs back together. He's like a child, flying his kite, constantly scribbling on the Memorial, solemnly pretending to understand grown-up affairs. He's childishly pleased when he completes a simple task, like the copy work he learns to do. But this makes a good balance for Betsey, with her snap judgments and muddled emotions. Because he is child-like, he responds to the world with pure instincts, and his opinions of people are usually right on target.

## Mr. Wickfield

The Wickfield house is always described as old and quaint, and Agnes' father is like a figure of old England—mellow, kindly, refined, but beginning to deteriorate. Mr. Wickfield is haunted by the past, especially by the memory of his wife, whom Agnes resembles so much. When he first appears, Mr. Wickfield is a competent lawyer, but he's already hesitant and melancholy. His gradual decay generally takes place offstage, described by Agnes, Uriah, or Micawber; somehow that makes it sadder and more helpless. Like Dan Peggotty, he lives for his daughter, but unlike Dan he cannot really rebuild his life. Though Heep's evil is rooted out, Mr. Wickfield refuses to return to work, living instead as a harmless white-haired gentleman near Agnes while she runs her school.

## Dr. and Mrs. Strong

The Strongs' name is ironic, for neither of them is strong. David's schoolmaster is good and kind but absentminded and too trusting. His young wife Annie is also goodhearted, but she has let her manipulative mother get her into difficult situations—first into marriage with an older man, then into a dangerous flirtation with her cousin Jack Maldon. When David first observes what is going on, he assumes that Annie is having an affair with Jack, and at that point her sexual temptation foreshadows Emily's seduction by Steerforth. However, later David learns that Annie has been faithful to the Doctor. Hearing her talk about how her love has deepened and matured gives him something to ponder in his own youthful marriage.

## Rosa Dartle

Mrs. Steerforth's companion Rosa Dartle is a troubling, ambiguous character. Like her cousin James, Rosa is haughty and contemptuous, but she hasn't got his charm to soften the superior air. Like Emily, Rosa apparently gave herself to Steerforth, but she's now cast-off and bitter, a warning for Emily. Like Jane Murdstone, Rosa becomes a dependent spinster whose emotions burst out in bizarre ways— her repressed love for Steerforth is like Jane's for her brother. Rosa is certainly a melodramatic figure—dark, intense, with a livid scar slashing across her lip where Steerforth attacked her. The scar is a constant reminder of Steerforth's cruelty, as well as a symbol of the blight on Rosa's soul. Her speech seethes with hidden meanings. In her showdown with Emily, she reaches such a pitch of emotion that it's hard to tell what she's feeling. Rosa is one of Dickens' most haunting characters, a disturbing reminder that not everyone lives happily ever after.

# Other Elements

## SETTING

*David Copperfield* is set in the years of Dickens' youth rather than at mid-century, when he wrote it, and therefore at least the first half of the novel is tinged with nostalgia. Readers in Dickens' own time recognized the clothing and customs described in the book as "old-fashioned." Dickens fondly recreated the era of stagecoaches, which he had ridden all over England as a young reporter covering stories. By 1850, however, railroads had transformed the country.

Along with its multiple plots, *David Copperfield* has multiple settings. The childhood settings are softened, charming, idealized. David is born in Blunderstone in Suffolk. (Dickens had found this suggestive name on a signpost.) The village is pictured vaguely because Dickens did not know Suffolk villages well, having been bred a city boy. Yarmouth, the seaside town where the Peggottys live, was more to his taste. After spending one day there, he caught its spirit and dialect so accurately that readers assumed he was from there. David's teenage years are spent in Dover and Canterbury, close to Dickens' happy early childhood home in Chatham. Seen through his fond memory, these towns are depicted lovingly.

But Dickens' greatest literary territory was London. For this book, he drew upon memories of his blacking-warehouse days, when wandering the streets for hours was the only entertainment he could afford. As David's adult home, it seems a more complicated and gritty place. Central London itself appears depressing, from the musty precincts of Doctors' Commons to the dark streets where Dan Peggotty hunts for Emily. David also travels far into the suburbs, visiting the Steerforths and the Strongs in Highgate, Dora at Norwood or Putney, and Traddles in shabby Camden Town.

The only houses described in detail are Dan Peggotty's eccentric boat-house and the Wickfields' quaint old home in Canterbury. David himself spends a lot of time on the road, in Barkis' cart, in coaches, or walking long distances. (Dickens was a great walker.) Where do you think David feels most at home?

## THEMES

### 1. THE MAKING OF A WRITER

Like many novels, *David Copperfield* shows its main character growing up. But since David is a writer, the lessons he learns are especially important for that profession. Consider this at each stage of David's development. Look for evidence in his childhood that he's destined to be a storyteller. Think about the importance he places on education and discipline. Watch for episodes where David is an observer of events, drinking in impressions of life rather than acting upon them. Think about how David's suffering deepens his art, and how his struggle to balance romantic and realistic outlooks may lead him to see all aspects of life.

## 2. MARRIAGE

This novel presents you with a spectrum of marriages. David himself is married twice and learns that romantic love and domestic happiness don't always come in the same package. Dickens looks at power struggles in married life. For example, compare Mr. Murdstone's tyranny over his wife to the Micawbers' loyal partnership. Dickens could not write openly about sex, but sexual currents run strongly beneath the surface. For example, think about Annie Strong married to old Dr. Strong, or Agnes pursued by vile Uriah Heep. Emily chooses an affair with the attractive Steerforth over marriage to Ham, whom she loves as a brother, yet David's brotherly love for Agnes appears more lasting than his attraction to Dora. Dickens shows some couples, like Peggotty and Barkis, making a go of unromantic marriages while he depicts others, like Aunt Betsey, as bitterly disappointed by romantic marriages.

## 3. DISCIPLINE

Dickens emphasizes discipline as a virtue David must cultivate. Aunt Betsey goes to great lengths to teach David self-reliance. Though he lacks David's talent, Traddles shows how far steady work alone can carry someone toward success. Useful work is a joy to Mr. Dick, and it transforms Mr. Micawber. Set against this, however, are those who abuse discipline, such as the Murdstones and Mr. Creakle. Dickens asks you to consider emotional discipline as well. David's romantic nature needs to be brought under control before he can find happiness. Steerforth and Emily lack discipline, and this leads them to ruin, whereas Annie Strong saves herself by disciplining her heart. In contrast, Aunt Betsey must learn to be less disciplined and more open to her feelings.

### 4.   PARENTS AND CHILDREN

Almost no one in this book has a complete family. There are orphans (Traddles, Ham, and Emily), only children with a single parent (Agnes, Uriah Heep, Steerforth), and only children with a single parent who later become orphans (David and Dora). Often these single parents have an unhealthy attachment to their children. Mrs. Steerforth ruins her son, Mr. Wickfield ruins himself for Agnes, Mrs. Markleham undermines her daughter's marriage, and Dan Peggotty becomes obsessed with searching for his adopted daughter. The only big, happy family is the Micawbers, and Dickens suggests that they have too many children. Dickens came from a large, poor family himself. The effect of these fragmented homes is to emphasize characters' loneliness, the fragility of the family, and the importance of forming other bonds of friendship and responsibility.

### 5.   ROMANCE VS. REALITY

As David struggles to balance these two strains

in his personality, consider other characters who relate to this theme: the romantics (Mrs. Copperfield, Emily, Dora, Steerforth, Mr. Wickfield, the Micawbers) and the realists (Aunt Betsey, Uriah Heep, Traddles, Agnes, the Strongs). Consider also how Dickens shifts between romantic and realistic viewpoints and styles.

## STYLE

Dickens is known for a rich range of writing styles—indignant, ironical, melodramatic, and sentimental, all of which appear in *David Copperfield*. To set the nostalgic tone for this novel, he also uses certain words like "little" and "old" more than usual, so his language seems especially sentimental. He tries to intensify the melodramatic impact with words such as "quite," "great," "very." These styles suit the Victorian fashion of emotional fiction, but they also reflect Dickens' personal habit of emotional involvement with his books.

The tone of *David Copperfield* is, of course, mostly controlled by its narrator. Sometimes David's narrative voice is exaggerated and ironical, as in the opening paragraphs. Yet because, as he says, these memoirs are not to be read by anyone else, he often speaks in an honest and straightforward tone of voice, as at the end of Chapter II. When he wants to show the older narrator's perspective on his younger self, he uses a tongue-in-cheek style, as when he describes David's infatuation with Dora.

There are many other voices in the novel, too, for Dickens is a superb dramatist: his characters reveal themselves more by what they say than by what he says about them. Compare Rosa Dartle's intense, sarcastic speeches to Steerforth's languid drawl. Read aloud examples of Mr. Micawber's pompous, wordy, euphemistic speeches, or Uriah Heep's winding, jerky, suggestive sentences.

## POINT OF VIEW

This novel is seen through the eyes of David Copperfield. This should limit the story to events David has witnessed, but Dickens gets around that. Often he will have another character tell a piece of the story in a speech to David (like Dan Peggotty's account of his search for Emily) or in a letter (like Emily's letters home). When Dickens needs to show a private scene, such as the Strongs' reconciliation or Rosa Dartle's accusation of Emily, he makes David happen to turn up so he can be a spectator. David even gives a detailed description of his own birth.

Often Dickens will let a dramatic scene play out, almost as if it were on stage, as with Peggotty's quarrel with Mrs. Copperfield in Chapter II. In other dialogue scenes, like Aunt Betsey's conversation with Mr. Chillip in Chapter I, Dickens steers your responses in a particular direction with loaded descriptions and comments. In general, however, David speaks directly to you. You can even picture him as he writes; for example, in the middle of a description he may stop to comment on how vividly he still sees it, or how the memory affects him. (He says the smell of geraniums always reminds him of falling in love with Dora.) He also comments on what he did not know at the time, handing you a clue to future events and pulling you forward in the story.

# FORM AND STRUCTURE

*David Copperfield* was written in twenty monthly installments (it actually came out in nineteen parts, the final one being a double installment). Each installment was written to fit thirty-two closely printed large pages. Dickens kept each of his subplots moving along each month, never leaving an important character offstage for too long. He also ended each installment on a note of suspense, surprise, or foreboding. Toward the end of the book, some readers feel that the climaxes of the different plots are clustered too closely. For example, David has to leave his dying wife's bedside to help expose Uriah Heep, and then he hardly has time to grieve for her death before he's off to watch Ham and Steerforth die. Some readers have also criticized the coincidences Dickens uses to keep his plots interconnected. But he believed that this imitated life, where events are jumbled together in surprising ways.

Here are several ways you can examine the book's structure:

1. As David grows up, the book's vision and style change. First comes the fairy-tale world of Suffolk and Yarmouth, which lasts until David runs away from the factory. Next comes the social comedy of David's adolescence, until Betsey is ruined. Then there is the melodrama of his adulthood, until Dora and Steerforth die. In the melancholy epilogue, David marries Agnes.

2. The book falls into two parts because Dickens has different motives for writing each half. First he is remembering his own childhood, up through

the time David goes to London. Then he starts writing a novel about the education of a novelist.

**3.**  This novel is divided into four parts by the four "Retrospect" chapters, XVIII, XLIII, LIII, and LXIV. Each retrospect catches David at a moment when he has achieved a goal or acquired new knowledge of the world—and will soon be moving on.

# The Story

Dickens wrote *David Copperfield* in monthly installments, each a few chapters long. Let's read the novel section by section, as it originally appeared.

## Chapters I–III

In the famous opening sentence, you learn at once that this is a first-person account. You also sense the narrator's uneasy modesty and ambivalence about himself. Suspense is set up—will he be the "hero" of this story? Why shouldn't he be? Who might be the hero(es) instead? Finally, you see the narrator as a writer, willing to let his writing answer these questions.

Almost as though he's unsure of himself, David makes a couple of false starts on his tale. First he records only the facts. Then he veers off into comical anecdotes about the neighbors' superstitions and the auction of his caul.

---

**NOTE:**   A caul is a piece of fetal membrane occasionally found on a baby's head at birth. Though it was considered good luck, David's birth hour was considered unlucky, so his prospects are already uncertain. A caul was said to protect against drowning; drowning will later play a significant role in the novel.

---

David gradually settles down into his story. He explains his father's early death and his quarrel with his rich aunt Betsey Trotwood. Then, having established the family circumstances, David launches into a direct dramatization of his birth day. In this comical scene, Aunt Betsey marches in, criticizes everything in the house, intimidates David's gentle mother Clara, and practically orders her to give birth to a girl. This sends Clara into labor. A second scene, in which Aunt Betsey treats mild Dr. Chillip the same way, confirms her character. When she learns that a boy has been born, she leaves abruptly, refusing to have anything to do with him. David is evidently not off to a good start.

---

**NOTE:** David couldn't have witnessed these scenes, since he wasn't born yet. He draws them from what he's been told. But his impulse to dramatize them—and his skill at doing so—helps you to see him as a convincing storyteller.

---

David shifts to another narrative style in Chapter II: detailed present-tense impressions of his daily life as a child. Though he makes you aware that he is a grown man remembering these things, he also attempts to recapture his childish perspective. He sees his mother and their servant, Peggotty, foreshortened as they stoop down to him. The chickens in the yard look huge, and the hallway seems terribly long. He uses all his senses, including touch (Peggotty's rough forefinger) and smell (the mouldy air of the pantry). He also recreates a child's fancies, for example in his wandering imagination during church services.

David shifts back to the past tense with a scene by the parlor fire with Peggotty. Dickens drew upon his memory of how it feels to stay up past your bedtime, as he makes sleepy David imagine Peggotty swelling in size. He fixes his heavy eyes on nearby objects—Peggotty's thread wax, her workbox with St. Paul's on the lid, and her brass thimble. Then the little boy begins an odd conversation with Peggotty about marriage. (Notice that David's first speech in the novel centers on this main theme.) Peggotty's anxious reaction tells you that this topic is sensitive for some reason. As you read the dialogue, you can guess that it concerns David's mother, and immediately she appears with a gentleman friend. When the man compliments David's mother, David instinctively becomes jealous. David has painted a picture of a charmed childhood; now a force enters to destroy it.

David records what is happening accurately, yet he doesn't seem to understand its significance. The same is true after the gentleman leaves, when Mrs. Copperfield and Peggotty argue. You can read these scenes on two levels: what David sees and hears, and what an adult would understand is happening.

Mr. Murdstone and Peggotty begin to represent

two opposing forces. David remembers seeing Mr. Murdstone more and more, while Peggotty is with them less and less. Whereas Peggotty huddles with David inside the house, Mr. Murdstone takes David out into the world, on horseback. David, who's been raised by women, now enters a man's world. Mr. Murdstone's friends at the hotel smoke cigars, drink, and joke crudely. Mr. Murdstone, however, comes off as a cold, commanding person.

---

**NOTE: David's names**   David, although he doesn't catch on, is called "Brooks of Sheffield" here because he's so sharp. Sheffield is a city famous for making sharp knives. Throughout the book, David will be given new names by various characters. As someone who's searching for an identity, he tries to live up to each of these names. Consider the meaning of these names as they appear.

---

David adds another ominous stroke to his portrait of his mother. When he innocently repeats the men's leering remarks, she's vain, excited, and flattered. Peggotty's invitation to David to go with her to Yarmouth follows quickly. Clearly this concerns getting David out of the way, but innocent David is eager to go. Simple sentences at the end of the chapter describe his departure poignantly. Yet Dickens adds an extra level of meaning by slipping in without comment details of the behavior of Mrs. Copperfield, Mr. Murdstone, and Peggotty, suggesting the power struggle that's going on.

At Yarmouth, David is charmed by Peggotty's brother's house—a barge lodged on dry shore, with a chimney, doors, and windows stuck in. He sees it as a fairy-tale place and admires how tidy and cunning everything is inside. At the same time you can see the barge from an adult's perspective—cramped, cluttered, fishy-smelling. The first time David describes the inhabitants, Ham, Em'ly, Mrs. Gummidge, and Dan Peggotty, he shows only their outsides, as any child would. But inside the house at night, as David feels its warmth and security (he compares it to Noah's ark), these characters come alive. Dickens poses them around the fire, as if in a sentimental painting.

---

**NOTE: Dialect**   Dickens records the Yarmouth dialect accurately in the speech of Daniel, Ham, and Mrs. Gummidge. Emily, however, speaks standard English. Dickens often uses dialect either for comic effect or to emphasize a character's social class. Sometimes Dickens uses dialect to emphasize the simple goodness of working-class people, like Dan and Ham. In other cases, he will use dialect to show that a villain is from the lower classes. As you read, notice who speaks dialect, and consider why.

---

In a conversation with Mr. Peggotty, David learns the family circumstances. Mr. Peggotty has generously taken in orphaned Ham and Emily and widowed Mrs. Gummidge. Their fathers and husband were all, as Mr. Peggotty aptly mispronounces it, "drowndead."

**NOTE: Foreshadowing** The next day, when Emily tells David about her fear of the sea and her desire to be a lady, Dickens is setting up the elements of her tragic fate. Some readers think this is heavy-handed, but others point out how little Dickens actually has David say. Young David accepts Emily's words without comment. When she runs out recklessly on the jetty, it's the older David who reflects that it might have been better if she had died then, and this only increases the suspense. Look for more foreshadowing, especially in reference to Emily, as the novel progresses.

David speaks whimsically of his childhood love for Emily, yet he makes it sweet, too, in its innocence. The ultimate test of this household's goodness is the way it accepts self-pitying, complaining Mrs. Gummidge. It's hard for David to tear himself away, though once he's headed for home, he looks forward to seeing his mother again. When he arrives, though, everything has changed. There's a new servant at the door. When Peggotty anxiously tries to explain that his mother has remarried, David at first leaps to the conclusion that she's dead. In fact, she might as well be dead, for when he goes to greet her in the parlor, she's so intimidated by Mr. Murdstone ("Control yourself!" he warns her) that she can't relate to her son in the old way. He flees to his bedroom, but even his belongings have been moved. Chapter III (and the first installment) ends with the image of the new dog in the kennel, a dog as threatening as Mr. Murdstone himself.

# CHAPTERS IV–VI

In Chapter IV, Dickens proves he was a master of child psychology before the science had even been established. David's mother comforts him behind her husband's back, but when Mr. Murdstone joins them, she gives in to his insistence on "firmness." Later, she hugs David in the dark, but she does it furtively. David, too, learns to lie, to tell his stepfather that the smudge on his face is dirt, not tears, in order to escape a beating. After the openness and generosity he found at Mr. Peggotty's house, David feels Mr. Murdstone is mean and harsh indeed.

---

**NOTE: Character Devices**   Dickens uses many techniques to "tag" characters. One way is to give them names that sound like their qualities. (Murdstone is a perfect example—the name sounds *murderous* and *hard*.) Another is to repeat phrases throughout a character's speech, like Mr. Murdstone's "firmness" or Mrs. Gummidge's "a lone lorn creetur." A third technique is to associate the character with objects. As Mr. Murdstone's sister is introduced, notice how many metallic objects surround her. Like metal, she is cold, hard, and heavy.

---

At the dinner table, Mr. and Miss Murdstone skillfully work together, manipulating Clara until she bends to their viewpoint. David feels a new spirit pervading his life. Compare the church scene in Chapter II with his gloomy visits now. David

explicitly compares his grueling lessons with Mr.
Murdstone to the pleasant ones he used to share
with his mother. He dramatizes his lessons by using the present tense, catching every wave of
miserable emotion that blocks his learning.

---

**NOTE:**   The one thing that saves David is reading
books he finds in the attic. These were the books
Dickens himself read and loved best as a child. An
early love of novels is a clue that David is destined
to be a writer.

---

One day Mr. Murdstone brings a cane to the
lessons, and the threat of being beaten drives
everything else from David's mind. (Note Mr.
Murdstone's sadistic touch—he makes up absurd
story problems about canes.) Though David has
become sullen and passive, at this showdown his
fighting spirit rises, and in the physical struggle
he instinctively bites Mr. Murdstone. Dickens
understood how natural a child's sense of guilt is.
After he's been beaten and locked away, David
feels like a criminal, the more so because he is
treated like one. Like a life force, Peggotty breathes
hope to him through the keyhole. But when David
is sent away to boarding school, his mother is not
allowed to say good-bye fondly. She's been persuaded he's wicked—and he feels he is, too.

Comedy blossoms in Chapter V, as a welcome
relief from the Murdstones. Peggotty's sly, de-
fiant, button-bursting farewell is comical. So is
David's dialogue with the inarticulate wagon-driver
Barkis, with his mysterious message for Peggotty,
"Barkis is willing." The waiter at the coach-stop

inn is also comical, with his friendly way of swindling innocent David out of his lunch. Nevertheless, the waiter's gruesome story of what happened to a boy at David's school (though he's probably just teasing David) plants a seed of worry in David's mind. At this point, what do you sense David is heading for?

The other coach passengers are satirized merrily, too. During the trip David imagines the lives in the villages they pass through (again, a writer's instinct). He sees London in terms of storybooks and, abandoned briefly at the coach office, he invents various fates for himself. The schoolmaster who finally picks him up isn't particularly friendly. But as that man visits his poor old mother, who so obviously loves him (even admiring his wretched flute-playing!), Mr. Mell becomes a sympathetic character.

Salem House looks desolate to David. It's square, plain, and empty of life. The boys are still on vacation—David's been sent here early as a punishment.

---

**NOTE:** Dickens gives you a description of the schoolroom which indirectly paints a picture of routine school life. It begins realistically with the layer of papers scattered over the floor, and ends in exaggeration as he imagines the skies raining ink on the room. In between are several unexpected details. The schoolroom pets suggest how bored and lonely the boys are. Dickens captures the peculiar smell of the room, too, pulling together images of school uniforms, smuggled snacks, unhealthy dampness, and stale air.

---

The detail that really defines the school is the sign David is forced to wear: "Take care of him. He bites." This is cruel and unusual punishment indeed, and it haunts David, taking over his self-image. In the dreary days that follow, David's fertile mind is filled with melancholy memories of home and apprehensive images of the other schoolboys, drawn imaginatively from names he's read carved in a door.

When school begins in Chapter VI, David discovers the rotten source of authority—Mr. Creakle. In his quarters (comfortable compared to the boys' rooms), the headmaster sits like an angry tyrant. His whispering voice is fierce with repressed energy, and the one-legged porter Tungay repeats what Creakle says in a louder voice, to heighten its bullying power. The boys, however, are better than David imagined. Traddles is kind, and helps make David's sign a simple joke. James Steerforth, clearly a leader and a hero, also saves David from shame, though at the same time he gets control over David's spending money. Even naive David is a little suspicious of Steerforth's offer, but the party that princely Steerforth throws with David's money is a genial, delightful affair. That night, David gets the inside story on sadistic Creakle, malicious Tungay, and the underpaid teachers Mr. Sharp and Mr. Mell. Steerforth's privileged position becomes clear, too. Before they go to sleep, Steerforth asks David if he has a sister. What does this suggest to you about Steerforth's character?

David is clearly attracted to Steerforth, as he watches the older boy, graceful and handsome in his sleep. Nevertheless, the older narrator drops a hint about the cloud he should have seen hanging over Steerforth—an ominous foreshadowing to end this installment.

# CHAPTERS VII–IX

Creakle takes sadistic pleasure in beating boys, as David learns the next day when he and several other boys are caned for no reason. In a series of present-tense sketches, David relives the anxiety of these daily beatings. You also see their effect on cheerful Tommy Traddles, and you see that Steerforth alone is above punishment. Then, however, David shows you a vulnerable side of Steerforth. Discovering that David has read many stories and can tell them well, Steerforth, who has trouble sleeping, persuades David to entertain him at bedtime. What do you think Steerforth's hunger for stories is a sign of? David doesn't really enjoy performing on call for him—he suspects that it encourages a harmful romantic streak in him. But he's flattered by the attention.

The bad side of Steerforth's character is shown in the next long scene. On a rainy afternoon the boys are so boisterous that long-suffering Mr. Mell shouts at them in exasperation. When Steerforth insolently talks back, Mr. Mell loses his temper, accusing Steerforth of corrupting younger students. (Mr. Mell seems to be referring to David, though he doesn't say so.) When Creakle intervenes, Steerforth reveals coolly what he has learned from David about poor old Mrs. Mell. Creakle unjustly fires Mr. Mell, ostensibly because he hid his poverty, but really because Creakle has to back Steerforth. Steerforth's conscience seems to trouble him, and he quarrels with Traddles for feeling sorry for Mr. Mell. David feels bad about it too, but he keeps silent.

Soon after, David gets a surprise visit from Mr. Peggotty and Ham. Notice how much older David seems—he relates to them more self-consciously. They speak often of Emily, who they say is growing up, too, becoming a woman. Then Steerforth strolls in, and David introduces them. They are charmed by Steerforth. But on some vague instinct, David decides not to tell Steerforth about Emily. At this point in the story, do you share David's opinion of Steerforth? Why?

David is eager to go home for the holidays, and the comic talk he has with Barkis on the way sets a happy, homey tone. But as David draws closer to the Rookery, his bad memories revive. The scene appears bleak and wintry. Then the sound of his mother's singing triggers a rush of earlier, happier feelings. When he runs in and discovers she has a new baby, he's delighted. To top it off, the Murdstones are gone for the day. David spends a happy afternoon, though he notices that his mother seems thinner, more anxious, and more dependent on Peggotty.

---

**NOTE:** Peggotty briefly mentions Aunt Betsey in this conversation. Remember that Dickens had to keep his characters "alive" through several installments. Betsey won't appear again in the plot for several chapters, but Dickens doesn't want you to forget who she is.

---

David's mother bickers with Peggotty about the

Murdstones. This is one way Dickens can bring you up to date on the state of things in that household without having David tell you outright. From the conversation you can tell that vain, pliant Clara has been brainwashed by her husband and sister-in-law. David picks up on some of this, but he doesn't find fault with his beloved mother—just as he has been unable to find fault with Steerforth.

When the Murdstones return, the mood of the house changes perceptibly. David avoids them that night, and he can hardly face going down to breakfast the next morning. But David isn't just being timid—he really is unwelcome. Miss Murdstone counts the days until he's due to leave. He isn't allowed near the new baby. He's criticized constantly, and he's made to feel conspicuous the moment he enters a room. A dramatized scene in the parlor shows you that the Murdstones are using their disapproval of David to gain more control over Clara, but David feels personally abused. If you've ever been caught in the middle of a family quarrel, you may know how he feels.

---

**NOTE: Rhetorical style**   At the end of Chapter VIII, Dickens uses his rhetorical style in a series of sentences beginning with "What" and ending with an urgent exclamation point, as David lists the torments of his vacation. In the third paragraph of this series, a string of clauses each ends miserably with the phrase "and that mine." And the final paragraph piles up "what's" frequently, desperately.

---

It's clear that David is glad to leave when his vacation is over. But he still loves his mother, and he's bitterly sorry for her.

---

**NOTE: Dickens' Cinematic Technique**    Dickens instinctively used cinematic techniques, though movies hadn't been invented in his time. Clara's anguish is crystallized here in a single, wordless moment—almost like a movie shot. She stands at the gate, intently holding up her baby; David's vision zooms in on her as he rides away. It's a mute cry from a doomed victim, more powerful than any speech could be.

---

The cold, foggy weather on David's next birthday suggests that something bad is about to happen. Weather is often an omen in Dickens' novels. David perks up when he's called to the school office, but Mr. Sharp is ominously kind. Mrs. Creakle tries to break the news gently, but David is bright enough to guess, before she's finished telling him, that his mother has died. Dickens' psychological insight helps him to trace realistically the stages of David's grief. After crying, David thinks not of his mother but of the trappings of death—her gravestone, their shut-up house, and his own role as a mourner. He even plays up his grief, enjoying the attention from the other boys.

Before he gets home, David has to stop off in Yarmouth to be measured for his mourning clothes. In contrast to the expected mood of death, Mr. Omer's undertaker's shop is a busy, merry place. Fat Mr. Omer, his daughter Minnie, and his coffin-maker Joram are quite used to funerals. Mr. Omer describes David's mother just as he'd describe any corpse, by the size of the grave, and Minnie and Joram flirt with each other as though they're on a picnic. But this seems ghoulish to David, and he assumes they're hardhearted.

There's plenty of grief at the Rookery. Peggotty attends her dead mistress almost obsessively. Even Mr. Murdstone is weeping, though Miss Murdstone is as cold and practical as ever. David describes her bitterly, but he shifts to a gentler, more sympathetic tone as he depicts Mr. Murdstone's restless, tight-clenched sorrow. In the present tense, David shows the full ritual of a Victorian funeral, a solemn religious affair. (Dickens uses no irony in writing about God, for he was a firm Christian.) It's like an old movie, silent except for the resounding words of the Lord.

---

**NOTE: A second narrator** David doesn't witness his mother's death, though Dickens could have written it so David got home in time to see her die. Instead he uses Peggotty to narrate the touching scenes. That way, he can keep death at a respectful distance. (Notice how he does this throughout the book.) As Clara's close friend and an adult, Peggotty can interpret her feelings better than David could. Also, by having Peggotty, with her strong, simple emotions, describe the death, Dickens can lend emotion to it without appearing too sentimental himself.

---

David consciously begins to idealize his mother as soon as she is dead. But oddly enough, he also pictures himself as her infant child, dead on her bosom. In a way, her death marks the end of one life for David—and the beginning of another, still to be defined.

# CHAPTERS X–XII

Once Clara is dead, the Murdstones fire Peggotty and ignore David. At first it's a relief to him to be left alone, but gradually he's disturbed by his solitude, sensing Mr. Murdstone's anger. (Do you think Mr. Murdstone's grief is a normal reaction? Does it fit in with your image of him?) Peggotty comes to the rescue and takes David to Yarmouth again. Their trip over with Barkis is more comical than ever, with the wagon-driver pressing his bizarre courtship of Peggotty. Barkis is not very romantic, crowding next to her on the seat and repeating, "Are you comfortable?", but afterwards Peggotty admits that she's thinking of marrying him. Her reasons are entirely practical—this way she can still be near David and near Clara's grave. Peggotty sees marriage in a different light than romantic Clara Copperfield did.

David seems older; the boat-house looks smaller to him, and his relationship with Emily is coyer, more sexual. Ham, too, clearly has an adolescent crush on Emily. In this charged atmosphere, it seems dangerous to have the conversation turn to glowing praise of Steerforth. David notices with a start how eagerly Emily is listening to it all. Side by side with these fragile, youthful emotions is Barkis and Peggotty's prosaic courtship.

---

**NOTE: Dickens' use of detail**   Dickens lists the presents Barkis brings Peggotty. Some—like the earrings or the canary—are typical lovers' gifts. Others are unromantic, like the dominoes and the pincushion. Others are totally inappropriate: oranges, apples, onions, pigs' feet, and pickled pork. By lumping these details together, Dickens shows that Barkis is a clumsy suitor, but he also gives a sense of real life, which is often an incongruous jumble.

David and Emily go with Barkis and Peggotty on their wedding trip. David flirts madly with Emily in the back seat, but considering how young he is, this only makes him look sillier than Barkis, who gets married with as little fuss and as much joy as possible. Marriage doesn't change Peggotty much. The very next day she brings David to her new house, to a room she'll always keep ready for him.

Back at the Rookery, David is still neglected. He's conscious that this is a waste of his mind (as was young Dickens when he was kept out of school). Again, books are his only pleasure. But bad as this situation is, worse follows. The narration pauses, while David makes a point of announcing the onset of a period of his life that will forever haunt him.

**NOTE:** Dickens' experience in the bootblacking factory scarred him deeply. As he begins to describe a similar episode in David's life, the horror of his own experience rises in his voice. But some readers feel that what happens to David isn't described with enough intensity to justify Dickens' tone of shock. (Compare this, for example, to Da-

vid's agony over wearing the sign at Salem House.)
Maybe Dickens recalled his past with such pain
that he couldn't accurately judge the impact of what
he had written.

One of the men David had met on his long-ago
ride with Mr. Murdstone shows up and hatches a
plan with Murdstone to send David to work in the
Murdstone & Grinby counting-house. Murdstone
claims this will help David improve his sulky temper. David is sharp enough to know that they're
just getting rid of him. As he rides away to London, uncomfortable in his stiff·trousers, and the
landmarks of home disappear, he looks blankly
upon his future.

David begins the next chapter by commenting
bitterly on how easily he was cast into this awful
life. He describes the counting-house objectively.
Yet in the same calm, almost sarcastic language,
he speaks of his agony, shame, tears. He claims
that no words can express that feeling adequately,
so he doesn't even try. Without dwelling on this
environment any further, he shifts gears to intro-
duce a comic character, Mr. Micawber, a lively mix
of shabbiness and pretentious airs. Smiling, friendly,
loquacious, he's an immediate bright spot in David's new life.

At the Micawbers' half-furnished house, David
meets Mrs. Micawber, who is also friendly, pretentious, and loquacious. She is always nursing a
baby in front of David. Like Dickens' mother, Mrs.
Micawber tries to keep a school for young ladies
but can get no pupils. The Micawbers are hounded
by creditors, just as the Dickenses were after they

moved to London. Dickens probably drew this all straight from his own life.

David gives an exact description of his finances, telling how he made his six or seven shillings' pay last for a week. (This would have been around two dollars. Although it would have gone further than two dollars would now, it is still far less than minimum wage levels today.) He becomes obsessed with food, probably because he can't afford much and is always hungry. Trudging into restaurants, wandering around the streets, he seems pathetically young and yet old.

---

**NOTE: Dickens' autobiography**   These passages are very similar to an autobiographical fragment Dickens wrote and gave to his friend John Forster. He's probably describing shops he went to and food he could still savor the taste of. This is effective, but a self-pitying, aggrieved, stuffy tone intrudes when Dickens begins to comment explicitly on his suffering. This is probably the attitude that earned Charles, as it earns David, the nickname "the little gent."

---

Once again, the bitter portrait of child laborers is superseded by welcome comedy in David's description of the Micawbers. David learns how to go to the pawnbrokers for them. When Mr. Micawber is sent to prison for debt (as Dickens' father was), David visits him there. It's a heavy experience for a little boy, but the Micawbers' liveliness makes it comic instead of tragic. Ironically, when Mr. Micawber is released from prison, both Mi-

cawbers are wretched, as though they need diffi-
culties to be happy.

David clings to the Micawbers' buoyant spirits
like a drowning swimmer to a life preserver. When
he learns they are moving away from London, he
feels abandoned and desperate. Going over his situation, he makes a decision. But he's learned to
be crafty: only after the Micawbers have actually
pulled away in the coach does he explain that he's
decided to run away to his Aunt Betsey, whom he
has imagined often from his mother's story of his
birth. He cleverly gets Peggotty to send him his
aunt's address plus some traveling money. Because he's conscientious, he finishes the week's
work he's been paid for, but he doesn't pick up
his next wages.

David has laid his plans carefully, but suddenly
everything goes wrong. The shifty young man he
hires to take his trunk to the coach-office runs away
with his belongings and gets Peggotty's half-guinea
away from him as well. David chases him fruit-
lessly. Nevertheless, he continues on the road to
Dover, miserable but determined to carry out his
plan. In his place, would you have done the same?
What alternatives does he have?

## CHAPTERS XIII–XV

**NOTE: Animated objects**  In Dickens' world, objects often seem to express the mood of the story.
Collapsing, exhausted, on the road that leads to
Kent, David sees a fountain that has "a great foolish image in the middle, blowing a dry shell"—a
fitting reflection of David's own foolish scheme.
Next he notices "feeble" candles burning at the

secondhand clothes shop, and trousers hanging from the ceiling like corpses—reflecting the desperation of David's walk to Dover. Watch for images like these in other scenes.

---

After selling his waistcoat for a few pennies, David sleeps on the ground outside his old school. This points up the reversal of his fortunes (and also deftly reminds you of Steerforth and Traddles). The next day he reaches Rochester and Chatham (towns where Dickens grew up and often took long walks himself). The clothes-seller David deals with there is even worse than the one in London, and you sense that David is sliding down in the world fast. The boy's innocent, shy manner traps him into dealing with this old lunatic, but he shows a promising stubborn streak in waiting outside the shop for hours until the old man forks over the money.

Dickens' prose reflects fascination and horror with the underworld of the open road. The tramps David sees are vicious: an itinerant tinsmith steals David's neckerchief, while his beaten-up girlfriend looks on helplessly. Once David gets to Dover, the boatmen, drivers, and shopkeepers joke callously when he asks for directions to his aunt's. Even when David finds someone who knows Aunt Betsey, the man's description of her is discouraging. Yet David presses on and at last finds her cottage—tidy and prosperous, in contrast to his own ragamuffin state. Intimidating as Betsey is, he approaches and speaks to her in a wavering, desperate, polite little voice. Then, as any child would, he bursts into tears.

As though in relief, the tone changes to broad

comedy. You see Aunt Betsey—awkward, confused, but concerned—lay David on a sofa and pour potions down his throat. The comedy increases as her permanent guest Mr. Dick "advises" Betsey on what to do with David. In a way she uses simpleminded Dick as a front, to conceal her kind intentions, but the fact that she's taken him in reveals her kindness even more. She looks mannish and acts gruff, chasing sightseers' donkeys off the green, but as David lies half-asleep she smoothes his hair gently. You get a feeling that David's found a home.

Next morning at breakfast, David and Betsey have a hard time communicating. In contrast, Mr. Dick readily confides to David his worries and ideas. Mr. Dick, however, obviously has mental shortcomings. He writes every day for hours on a long document about his affairs—the "Memorial"—but he can't help filling it with nonsense about King Charles I, who was beheaded two centuries earlier. Then he turns the useless manuscript into huge kites, to waft the facts away. David learns that Betsey saved this loveable lunatic from the asylum, and she staunchly defends his sanity. Betsey is obviously a good friend to those she loves.

Aunt Betsey has announced that she's writing to Mr. Murdstone about David, but it's Miss Murdstone who first appears, riding a donkey toward the green as if she knew it would annoy Betsey. The clash between these two willful, strong females begins with a tussle over the donkey. When they sit in the parlor to discuss David's fate, hostility crackles in the air. Betsey even guards David behind a chair, as if he were in physical danger. The conversation is masterly, like a game of poker.

Mr. Murdstone and Betsey sound each other out about David, testing, bluffing, and calling each other's cards. Mr. Murdstone has his vicious, agitated sister backing him up; Betsey has obedient, straightforward Mr. Dick. The Murdstones' repressed, formal coldness is no match for Betsey's shoot-from-the-hip style. Now that she's met the Murdstones, of course, Betsey is more than ever on David's side. (At what point do you feel she's made her decision?) To seal his fate, David makes an emotional speech, begging not to be sent back with the Murdstones.

---

**NOTE: Indirect speech**   In the middle of this lively dramatic dialogue, David's outburst is not quoted directly. Instead it's reported by the narrator. Dickens sometimes uses this technique to give you the impression of extreme emotion, as though he is delicately stepping back from it. He also uses indirect speech to contrast two verbal styles—here, the adults' formal negotiations against the child's heartfelt cry.

---

Betsey tells off Mr. Murdstone and, knowing how to infuriate her, ignores Miss Murdstone. The Murdstones leave in a huff. David is given a new name—Trotwood—and a new suit of clothes, and his new life begins. Once more, almost compulsively, he mentions the factory; then he buries it forever.

In Chapter XV David becomes a child again. He flies kites with the childlike grown-up, Mr. Dick, and he is enrolled in school. In Canterbury, Betsey takes him to Mr. Wickfield, the lawyer who will get David into the right school. But at the Wickfields', the first person David meets is the clerk Uriah Heep, a cadaverous-looking young man who comes out of the quaint, old house like a grim image of death. Inside, David meets Mr. Wickfield, who's pleasant but getting stout and red-faced. Then he meets Mr. Wickfield's daughter Agnes, who also seems unnaturally old. She's matronly and calm in her role as housekeeper, though she's only David's age. While her father looks like an aged version of his portrait, she already resembles her mother's portrait, only younger. David gets an image of her on the old oak staircase, looking like a stained-glass window—an old, saintly kind of art.

Betsey gives David some sound, almost fatherly parting advice, then quickly scuttles home, as though to hide her tears. At dinner with the Wickfields, David perceptively notices how much Mr. Wickfield dotes on Agnes, but also how melancholy that makes him, and how anxious Agnes is to cheer him up. David also notes Mr. Wickfield's tendency to drink too much. Canterbury looks like a lovely, quaint old town to David, but he can see the flaws in this antique setting. His final impression, too, is of Uriah Heep, with his clammy handshake and his watchful stare. How does Uriah's presence affect your feelings about Canterbury and the Wickfields?

## CHAPTERS XVI–XVIII

Like the rest of Canterbury, Dr. Strong's school is a grave, old-fashioned place, and Dr. Strong himself is disheveled and out of touch. His young wife Annie hardly seems to belong there; David at first thinks she's Dr. Strong's daughter. Mr. Wickfield holds an ambiguous conversation with Dr. Strong about finding a position for his wife's cousin Jack Maldon. What does this suggest to you? David doesn't try to interpret this situation. The other schoolboys he meets are merely idealized, happy students—David doesn't really describe them. He's too busy focusing on his reaction to them. His factory experience has set him back in learning, but aged his personality, so he doesn't feel at ease with kids his age. Agnes, however— an odd mixture of young and old herself—is a comforting companion for him.

Next you meet insolent Jack Maldon. He intrudes on the Wickfields' dinner, pressing Mr. Wickfield to find him a job nearby instead of abroad (which Mr. Wickfield seems to prefer, for Annie's sake. Why?). This triggers a note of uneasiness that deepens as, in a melancholy way, Mr. Wickfield asks David to live with them. Even more unsettling is David's conversation with Uriah Heep that night. This scene establishes Uriah's characteristics—his writhing, his fawning, his devotion to his mother, and his favorite word, "umble" (a lower-class pronunciation of "humble"). Future developments are hinted at, with Uriah's talk of becoming a partner and his admiration of Agnes. There's another bit of foreshadowing, too, when David dreams of Heep carrying him and Little Em'ly off in a pirate ship to be drowned.

Dr. Strong's school is an ideal, the exact opposite of Salem House. Dr. Strong is endearing, though absentminded, and girlish Annie Strong is sweet, although she sometimes acts as if she's guilty about something. David gives us a capsule caricature of

her silly, meddling mother Mrs. Markleham, nick-
named the Old Soldier. Then, in the scene of Jack
Maldon's going-away party, Dickens uses his dramatic skills to show us how these characters inter-
act. Jack flirts shamelessly with Annie, while the
Doctor smiles vaguely at Mrs. Markleham's crass
account of the Strongs' marriage. How do you feel
about this marriage? What elements in this scene
form your opinion?

---

NOTE: Dramatic details   David is too young to
understand this situation, but Dickens drops dramatic hints. Annie is agitated during her mother's
story, and Mr. Wickfield stares at her intently. She
won't sing or play cards, but she keeps moving
away when Jack Maldon sits beside her on the sofa.
As in a movie, the people's actions express their
emotions. David notices "something cherry-col-
ored" in Maldon's hand as he rides away. He
doesn't connect this with the ribbons on Annie's
dress, but you should. Then Mrs. Markleham notices a ribbon is lost, and Annie flushes. It looks
damning, and because you're not told anything
more definite, you can leap to your own conclusions about what Annie's up to.

---

After the party, David glimpses Dr. Strong in
his study, Annie sitting at his feet with a strange
expression on her face. This picture confuses David
but he records it carefully, adding suggestively that
it will be explained in a later chapter.

David receives a letter from Peggotty, updating
him on several old friends, and reminding you of

characters that are temporarily offstage. But right now David's more concerned with his new friends. Mr. Dick tells David a troubling story about a man who's been hanging around Betsey's gate, taking money from her. By choosing Mr. Dick to relate this scene, instead of his intelligent narrator David, Dickens gives you a fragmented, mysterious view of it. This dialogue also shows that Mr. Dick is loyal to Betsey, but can't help her when she's in trouble. How does this modify your sense of their household? More cheerfully, David describes Mr. Dick's visits to him at school, showing how he relates as an equal both to the boys and to Dr. Strong.

Another new friend, Uriah Heep, invites David home with him. Hiding behind his slithery humility, Uriah manipulates David, contradicting his polite remarks, turning his words around until David sounds pompous. At the Heeps' house, the bond between mother and son is uncanny. Like Mr. and Miss Murdstone, they skillfully work together in conversation. Somehow they pry all kinds of personal information out of David, until he's rescued almost magically by Mr. Micawber.

---

**NOTE: Coincidence**  Have you ever run into an old friend in a totally unexpected place? Simple coincidences like this help Dickens tie his plots together. This chance meeting will eventually make Micawber a key figure in Uriah's affairs. To some readers it seems preposterous that Micawber shows up in the same town as David, but Dickens claimed coincidences like this were quite common. Whether or not it's realistic, Dickens uses this coincidence to great literary advantage. He juxtaposes two total opposites—secretive, fawning Heep and trusting, self-confident Micawber—to define both their characters.

In this scene, David is in agony, caught between a sensitive fear of his past and shame that being accepted by Heep matters so much to him.

**NOTE: Caricature**  Characters like David, Betsey, Agnes, and Emily have realistic feelings and may change through their experiences. Characters like the Micawbers and the Heeps are one-dimensional caricatures who always behave the same. But this doesn't mean they're boring. The rest of this chapter shows David visiting the Micawbers, and you see all their characteristic gestures, phrases, and themes again. Dickens seems to love making them perform, almost like clockwork, exactly as you'd expect them to. Like some characters on television comedies, they have their own "bits" that they repeat in predictable situations, week after week. Does this make you laugh? Why?

Chapter XVIII is the first "Retrospect" chapter, in which David sums up a period of his life. Here, in present-tense descriptions, he grows up before your eyes— progressing in school, hating girls, getting into fights, having teenage crushes. Agnes is a constant presence, yet he seems to forget her whenever another girl is in the picture. David's lightly mocking tone reminds you, however, that he's reflecting on it as an adult, and now he knows how silly these romantic attitudes were. What does this suggest about how he feels about Agnes?

# CHAPTERS XIX–XXI

How do most people you know at school feel about graduation? When David graduates, he's sorry to leave school, but he's excited about seeing the world. He hasn't really thought about a career, except in romantic notions, but Aunt Betsey suggests it's time for him to choose one. She tells him that she wants him to become a "firm fellow." Betsey's idea of firmness, though, concerns strength of character, not the rigid repression of the Murdstones.

Before setting out for London, David says goodbye to Agnes. Their conversation shows their relationship—bantering, affectionate, but with an undercurrent of deeper feeling. It also brings out a new plot development: Mr. Wickfield's recent decline. Subtly, by having Agnes mention Uriah once, Dickens implies what David doesn't know yet—that Heep is partly behind this. Another worrisome note is sounded at the Strongs'. Jack Maldon has written from India, dropping hints that he wants to come home. David is old enough now to suspect an affair between Annie and Jack, and to feel, as does Mr. Wickfield, that Annie is a bad influence on Agnes. Does this fit in with your impression of Agnes' character?

David's journey by coach to London reverses his long-ago walk to Dover. Now, in contrast, he's riding in comfort, and it makes him a little conceited. But he's still fairly innocent. He's cheated out of his seat by a shifty-looking horse breeder, and the waiter at the inn in London passes off inferior food and wine on him. David is dazzled by the plays he sees at the theater that night. Soon after, he runs into his old friend Steerforth at the inn. Steerforth's opinion of the same performance is bored and jaded. It's a typical Steerforth attitude, of course, bringing him back into the story in familiar fashion. But it's also typical that Steerforth takes care of David, getting him a better room. No wonder David's dreams that night mix up Steerforth and the gods.

Next to Steerforth, David suddenly feels very young. Knowing that he doesn't shave much yet, he's embarrassed by the chambermaid's giggles as she brings his shaving water in the morning. The waiter acts respectful now, because Steerforth is in command. Steerforth gives David a new name— Daisy, signifying how girlish and naive he seems. The Steerforths' house at Highgate, where David visits, awes him, too. It's stately, dignified, and genteel, as is Mrs. Steerforth. Mrs. Steerforth's companion, Rosa Dartle, a poor relative, also intimidates David.

---

**NOTE: Characterization by speech** Dickens uses Rosa's way of speaking to define her character. Her swift wit shows you she's bright and perceptive, but her jerky, short phrases suggest a personality torn by conflicting impulses. Questions and exclamations give her speech energy, but in pretending to sound innocent she comes across as sarcastic, cynical, even vicious. You get an impression of an unhappy, frustrated woman, whose bottled-up resentment will erupt someday. While some readers view her with sympathy, others regard her as a potential source of trouble.

---

Rosa constantly reminds you of the unhappiness in this household. When David invites Steerforth to join him on his visit to the Peggottys, Rosa provokes Steerforth into callous remarks about "that sort of people." The scar that cuts across her lip is a constant reminder of Steerforth's careless temper. This sense of a taint over the household also colors Mrs. Steerforth's devotion to her son. Mrs. Steerforth, whose chief sin is pride, adores her son so much that she can't see him clearly, and she encourages him in his own pride. Notice how she goes on and on when she talks to David about James. David's replies are quoted indirectly, as if she's not even listening to him. Like Mr. Wickfield or Mrs. Heep, she seems too attached to her child, fatally obsessed with him.

---

**NOTE: Caricature** Dickens introduces Steerforth's manservant, Littimer, in Chapter XXI. Without saying so, Dickens makes you suspect this man's a villain. He's too quiet, almost sneaky, and hisses when he speaks. What other physical details of Littimer seem evil to you? Why? Dickens tags him repeatedly as "respectable," but his tone is ironic, so you can guess that this respectable appearance is not all there is to him.

---

Littimer makes David feel more like a boy than

anyone, and Steerforth is dangerously dependent upon him. This sets up an uneasy mood as Steerforth arrives with David in Yarmouth. At first Steerforth casually drops out of sight. David renews his acquaintance with the undertaker Mr. Omer, whose liveliness now appears simply genial. Emily works in his shop, and David learns from him the local opinion of her—that she puts on ladylike airs. David sees her through a doorway, but she's so beautiful that he's too shy to speak to her. Although she was once his sweetheart, she now seems in another world from David, and not necessarily for the better.

David visits his devoted Peggotty and the invalid Barkis, who has become a miser. Steerforth is so charming when he meets Peggotty that she adores him at once (compare this to Mrs. Steerforth's acceptance of David). After dinner, David and Steerforth go to the boat-house. But now it's dark and the wind sighs dismally. The older David who narrates this comments bitterly that he didn't realize that Steerforth considered this a game. Also ominous is Steerforth's comment that he found the house this morning "by instinct," almost like a predator sniffing out his prey. As David opens the door, a happy family scene is captured for a moment; a joyous announcement has just been made. But the happiness dissolves when David and Steerforth enter. Of course, they're greeted eagerly, and inarticulate Mr. Peggotty explains, though it takes a while, that Ham and Emily have just become engaged. His narration of their courtship depicts simple, honest emotions, growing slowly and steadily over time. But notice that Emily has run, ashamed, from the room, and even David feels a vague twinge of regret.

Steerforth is able, however, to put everyone at ease, even Mrs. Gummidge. Though Emily shrinks away from Ham, she listens raptly to Steerforth as he tells of a shipwreck (more foreshadowing). Walking away later, David is surprised by Steerforth's cold remarks that Ham is not good enough for Emily. David can't fit this in with Steerforth's sociable manner. He's still too innocent and trusting to read his friend's motives. Do you share David's view of Steerforth at this point? If not, what evidence in the book makes you feel differently about him?

# CHAPTERS XXII–XXIV

Why does David dwell on how often he and Steerforth were apart at Yarmouth? While David nostalgically relives the past, Steerforth is mysteriously absent. One evening, when David rejoins Steerforth at the Peggottys' house, Steerforth is sitting alone morosely by the fire, making obscure comments about how little moral guidance he has had, and what a torment he is to himself. He quickly cheers up, however, and tells David that he has bought a boat to keep moored at Yarmouth. David assumes Steerforth has done this as a kindness to Mr. Peggotty, but Steerforth is suspiciously embarrassed by this assumption. It also seems suspicious that Littimer has come down to help rig the boat out, and that Steerforth has named the boat the "Little Em'ly." When Emily and Ham arrive, she blushes as she greets Steerforth, then walks away from Ham. A mysterious woman follows Emily in the shadows, completing an unsettling picture.

At the inn, Steerforth introduces David to Miss Mowcher, a dwarf who's a hanger-on of high society. Her tag word is "volatile." Like Rosa Dartle or Uriah Heep, Miss Mowcher has a roundabout, insinuating manner of speech. She peppers this with fashionable slang and malicious gossip. Steerforth, too, makes breezy jokes, but David scarcely opens his mouth. Miss Mowcher, a manicurist and hairdresser, also seems to get involved in her clients' love lives, so she pays close attention to Steerforth's light talk of Emily. When David is asked to describe Emily, he makes a priggish little speech about her virtues. He seems out of his element with this worldly pair.

Later that night, David watches a melodramatic scene in the Barkises' kitchen. Emily talks with the young woman who followed her—a local girl, Martha Endell, who's lost her virginity and is now a figure of shame. Emily gives Martha money so she can go to London and be anonymous. Martha keeps repeating to Emily, "I was once like you!"— reminding you that Emily, too, could end up like this. After Martha leaves, Emily cries, saying she hasn't been good enough lately.

---

**NOTE: Sexual prudery**    In keeping with Victorian literary standards, Dickens never writes explicitly about sexual matters. Sometimes you have to read between the lines to figure out what's going on. You're only told vaguely of Martha's shame, though her "bold," "flaunting" looks suggest she's morally loose. Who was Martha's seducer? How did her affair become public knowledge? Is she pregnant? Dickens never answers such questions. Martha is just a figure of a fallen woman who foreshadows Emily's fall. Paired with the scene with

Miss Mowcher, this scene shows the double standard of Victorian society, where rich people fool around casually but the poorer classes are bound by strict moral codes.

---

On the coach back to London, David discusses his search for a career with Steerforth. But Steerforth merely points out the window at the flat landscape, suggesting that that's all he sees in life. When David mentions his aunt's suggestion that he become a proctor, Steerforth delivers a capsule satire of Doctors' Commons, where the proctors operate. David, however, knows Steerforth well enough not to take his cynicism seriously, and that night in London he tells his aunt that he likes the idea. Betsey speaks movingly to David about her love for him, and her regret for past mistakes. She also halts, briefly, in talking about the claims upon her income. This should stir your memory of the man Mr. Dick saw. The next day, on their way to Doctors' Commons, David and Betsey run into that man, who looks poor and ill-tempered. Betsey briefly goes away with him, but refuses to discuss this incident with David.

Spenlow and Jorkins' office in Doctors' Commons is described impressionistically: dusty, faded, with great bundles of papers and thick books piled high. Stiff, formal Mr. Spenlow is gracious to Betsey and David, but he seems restricted in his dealings by his rigid partner, Jorkins. David tells you that he later discovered that Jorkins was mild and timid, and Spenlow only used him as a front. Perhaps you should already be suspicious of Doctors' Commons.

**NOTE:** David's visit to the courtrooms of the
Commons gives Dickens an opportunity to satirize
this institution. Notice his satiric style: he pretends
to be ignorant, describing everything in literal terms
(the dining room chairs, the judge looking like an
owl). This strips away the court's dignity, and also
shows what a fraud it is. Dickens' objective, innocent tone is convincing because he seems like
an ordinary fellow with no particular axe to grind.

Romantic David likes this dreamy atmosphere,
however, and is also thrilled with the rooms Aunt
Betsey rents for him nearby, though the landlady
Mrs. Crupp looks shifty. Aunt Betsey keeps telling
David that he must learn to be firm and self-reliant, but he's so wrapped up in old memories of
the neighborhood and dreams of his new life that
he's hardly listening.

David says over and over how "fine" his situation is, but soon loneliness catches up with him
(the first person he misses is Agnes). He even has
dinner with Mrs. Steerforth and Rosa, so hungry
is he for company. Steerforth shows up soon, but
he has a busy social life. To be included, David
offers to throw a housewarming dinner party for
Steerforth and his college friends. David's tone is
heavily ironic as he remembers his foolish prepa-
rations. Mrs. Crupp takes advantage of him, per-
suading him to hire two useless servants, to order
more food than necessary (which she then steals),
and to order food already cooked so she won't
have to do any work. But David is delighted with
it all, though he's intimidated by Steerforth's so-

phisticated, affected friends. As the evening rushes by, David goes through every phase of drunkenness. He starts out bubbly, then becomes loud and talkative, then quarrelsome, then maudlin. He takes snuff and smokes; he has to stick his head out a window; he falls down the stairs in the dark. His loss of control is reflected by the way he describes himself as another person doing all this. His sentences get shorter and muddled. Finally, at the theater, he makes a complete fool of himself in front of Agnes, and this awakens his conscience. Steerforth gets him home to bed at last. The next morning, the pain of his hangover is nothing compared to his remorse and shame. Have you ever felt this kind of sinking feeling, realizing how you lost your self-control and made a fool of yourself "the night before"?

## CHAPTERS XXV–XXVII

Agnes' note to David the next day throws him into a tizzy. The trouble he takes in writing a reply shows his insecurity—with each attempt, he tests a different identity—but it also shows a writer's sensitivity to words, tone, and nuance. When he goes to meet her, he's relieved that she doesn't scold him. However, she warns him against Steerforth's influence. David stubbornly insists that Steerforth is not so bad, though in his heart he agrees with her. Then Agnes tells David of Uriah's growing hold on her father and his imminent partnership. David's dislike for Uriah is as strong as his love for Steerforth. Agnes, however, begs him to be civil to Uriah, for her father's sake, and bursts out crying in a rare moment of vulnerability.

Agnes' hostess, Mrs. Waterbrook, invites David to a fashionable dinner party. At this period in his life, Dickens had been honored with too many such parties, so he has David satirize the guests with exaggeration and irony. He uses capital letters scornfully to emphasize their favorite topics—especially Blood (meaning hereditary social position). Mr. Gulpidge and Mr. Spiker carry on an obscure conversation using initials instead of names, as if to confuse anyone who's not an insider. David is rather insignificant in this crowd, and he acts mostly as an observer. But he does meet his old Salem House friend Tommy Traddles, who's now a lawyer.

David makes a grudging effort at the party to be civil to Uriah Heep, even when Uriah follows him home. David is aware that he's brusque with Uriah and claims that he's too young to hide his disgust. (Do you agree with David that most adults learn to be hypocrites for the sake of "good manners"?) But Heep feeds on David's irritation, and spins out his description of Mr. Wickfield's growing incapacity as though to torment David. Uriah finishes by saying that he hopes to marry Agnes, using her father's dependence to force her to accept him. David listens, calmly, but he's revolted by the thought, and has a violent urge to run a fire-poker through Uriah.

---

**NOTE: Uriah and Agnes** Uriah and Agnes appear almost like two different species. Agnes seems all soul and character. David calls her his Angel, and when she gives him her hand, it seems like a precious object, not a warm, living hand. Uriah, however, is strongly physical. David calls him a "red-headed animal," and compares him to a dog, a fish, or a snake. When David takes his hand to lead him up the dark stairs, it feels like a damp, cold frog. David constantly describes Uriah's body movements, and when he watches him sleeping that night, Uriah is snoring grossly. How is this designed to make you feel about Uriah's intentions for Agnes?

---

Later, David reflects on the situation and worries that Agnes might give herself to Uriah, for her father's sake. Compare David's concern here to his blindness in regard to Steerforth and Emily. Perhaps David is more jealous of Agnes than of Emily, though he doesn't realize it. Maybe his love for Steerforth blinds him, while his hatred for Uriah opens his eyes.

David's daily life still seems lonely. Feeling sorry for himself, he writes scraps of romantic verse. After he's invited to Mr. Spenlow's house, he soaks up the clerks' extravagant notions about the boss's house. On the way down he listens dutifully to Mr. Spenlow's pompous talk about the Commons (Dickens gives David a bit of satire here). But as they approach the house, David pictures Miss Spenlow walking in the garden. When he learns her name is Dora, he thinks it's beautiful. David is ripe for romance.

David literally falls in love at first sight, picturing Dora like a creature of myth—"She was a Fairy, a Sylph." He doesn't tell you what she really looks like, except to say she is little and bright-eyed. Even the unexpected presence of Miss Murdstone, who is Dora's paid companion, can't faze David. She seems to have lost her power and is more anxious than David to bury their differences. But love is a torment: David is jealous of everyone around Dora, and he can't eat or carry on a conversation. When he sees himself in a mirror, he thinks he looks like an idiot.

---

NOTE: Dickens writes in an exaggerated, emotional voice, spouting clichés, to mock a young man's infatuation. His sentences are short and fragmented, much like the sentences in Chapter XXIV when David was drunk—implying that the two states of mind are similar.

---

Next morning, in the garden, David listens while Dora talks. Dickens has slanted David's perspective deliberately, to make you skeptical of David's beloved. You hear her chattering to her lapdog Jip. But whether or not Dora is a worthy object of love, David's emotions must be taken seriously (the smell of geraniums still triggers this dizzy delight in him years later, he says). After the weekend visit ends, thoughts of Dora take over David's life. He walks miles to Norwood just to catch a glimpse of her. Though he thinks he's being discreet, he's so smitten that even Mrs. Crupp notices it and is drunkenly sympathetic. This mortifies David, of course, for like any young lover he's painfully self-conscious.

In the next chapter David takes a break from love to visit Tommy Traddles. Impoverished, sloppy Camden Town reminds David of the Micawbers.

At the door of the house where Traddles lodges, a milkman is demanding to be paid, another echo of the Micawber days. Therefore, it isn't surprising that Traddles' landlords turn out to be the Micawbers, popping into David's life again.

In contrast to the Micawbers, Traddles seems sane and steady. He's not touchy about his shabby poverty; he remembers only the good things about Salem House; he works hard and has a realistic view of his talents. Like David, he is in love, although his sturdy, practical attitude is much different from David's romantic one. Traddles cheerfully accepts the prospect of a long engagement, and buys furniture one item at a time, telling himself it's a start. In what ways do you think Traddles' friendship might benefit David?

---

**NOTE: Characteristic speech**  By this time you can recognize Mr. Micawber's way of speaking, and enjoy hearing new variations on it. Look at this speech: "It was at Canterbury where we last met. Within the shadow, I may figuratively say, of that religious edifice immortalized by Chaucer, which was anciently the resort of Pilgrims from the remotest corners of—in short, in the immediate neighborhood of the Cathedral." The pretentious words ("edifice" instead of "building"), the literary allusions, and the way the sentence gets breathlessly off track until it falls apart ("in short"), are all typical of Micawber. The next-to-last paragraph of this chapter is an incredible burst of Micawber rhetoric, ending this installment with an energetic flourish.

---

# CHAPTERS XXVIII–XXXI

This installment begins pleasantly, as David has the Micawbers over for dinner. David has learned from experience; this time the dinner is reasonably simple. Although he's still intimidated by Mrs. Crupp and her tricks, he can handle the other servants now. The Micawbers and Traddles are delightful guests. Mr. Micawber expertly mixes the punch, and when Mrs. Crupp's mutton arrives half raw he grills the meat over the fire. Dickens' description of the food is so vivid you can almost taste it, and the gypsy-like gaiety of the meal makes it even better. But then Littimer arrives seeking Steerforth, and a chill quenches the fun. The meat he grills for them doesn't taste nearly as good as it did before. It's also unsettling that Steerforth apparently has vanished. Mr. Micawber regains his spirit enough to make a toast, but as he discusses his prospects, reasonable and hopeful as they sound, you've heard it too often before to believe it. Then the drink takes its effect. Mrs. Micawber lies down in the other room, David blushingly toasts Dora, Mrs. Micawber sings, and everyone gets sentimental. At the end of the evening, David pulls Traddles aside and wisely warns him not to lend Micawber money, but generous Traddles has already done so. Things seem out of control.

When Steerforth bursts in late that night, he's as charming as ever. But this good impression quickly sours, first when he carelessly forgets who Traddles is, next when he says he's been at Yarmouth on an "escapade." He brings a letter from Peggotty which tells David that Barkis is dying, but Steerforth regards this sad news callously. David sees a desperate, doomed look about his friend, and once or twice Steerforth looks at him oddly, silently. What do you think he's trying to tell David? After he's left, David remembers a letter Mr. Micawber slipped him earlier. It's a verbose, dramatic letter, admitting that Micawber is hopelessly in debt. (This spells doom for Traddles, too.) The evening started well, but ends in gloom.

Visiting Steerforth's home the next day, David feels Rosa Dartle watching him like a vulture. When she gets him alone, she asks piercing questions about Steerforth's mysterious absences. Later, she also hints that James and his mother may be heading for a serious falling-out. Suspense and melodrama build. Steerforth makes an effort to charm Rosa, and she does soften. She even plays her harp and sings, but her singing is unearthly and weird (compare it to Dora's doll-like chirping). Late that night, Steerforth demands a strange pledge from David, as though begging forgiveness in advance for some wrong he's about to do. David's last glimpse of his friend is of him lying gracefully asleep, as at school. David ends the chapter on a note of foreboding, saying that he would never touch Steerforth's hand again.

David heads next for Yarmouth, where, at Mr. Omer's, he catches up on the town's view of the Peggottys' lives. Mr. Omer remarks that Emily seems restless, anxious, now that her marriage to Ham is drawing nearer. Thus warned, when David sees Emily at the Barkises', he notices how frantically she clings to her uncle.

---

**NOTE: Sexual undercurrents**  David remarks that Ham has the soul of a gentleman, but is that enough for Emily? You'll have to decide for yourself what the undercurrent of emotion means. Is she frightened by the idea of marriage to Ham? Is she already guilty about Steerforth? Is there something unnatural in her attachment to her uncle? Dickens deliberately leaves you in troubling uncertainty.

---

Upstairs, David sees the dying Barkis, hugging his money box with his last strength. Though he's a feeble old miser now, as they watch him slip away, he regains his old comic identity—his last words are, "Barkis is willin'!" He dies as the tide goes out, just as Dan Peggotty had predicted. Yarmouth people have an uncanny relationship with the sea.

---

NOTE: Remember the string of gifts Barkis bought Peggotty when he was courting? There's another strange conglomeration of objects in Barkis' treasure box, everything from hay and an old horseshoe to money and stocks. The delusions of the man's whole life are collected there, from the child's miniature tea set, to the watch he wore on his wedding day, to the oyster shell he hoped to polish into a pearl. As David remembers how Barkis lugged this box around, pretending it was someone else's, a pathetic portrait of the miser emerges.

---

David is busy (and a little self-important) in reading the will and helping Peggotty with funeral arrangements. He sees nothing of Emily and Ham, though he hears their wedding date has been set for two weeks away.

David halts now, dreading the memory of the

events he's about to narrate; his emotional tone heightens the suspense. Then, in deliberately plain language, he sets the scene of his final night in Yarmouth. After a day of dreamy wandering, David is to meet the Peggottys at the boat-house. When he gets there, it looks cozy. Dan greets David heartily, Mrs. Gummidge moans and groans as always, and Dan, with childish pleasure, lights a welcoming candle in the window for Emily. But perhaps Dan goes on a bit too much about his devotion to Emily, saying he plans to keep the candle in the window even after she's married. He looks up eagerly as the door opens, but it's only Ham. And Ham is dressed in raingear, for a storm is rolling up. Ham gets David outside on a ruse, only to break down crying and announce that Emily has run away.

David frames Ham's anguished figure in his mind like a picture. A moment later, he fixes a picture of Mr. Peggotty's stricken face looking outside and grasping what's happened. Melodrama keeps rising; inside, there's wailing and crying, and Mr. Peggotty looks wild. David reads aloud Emily's passionate, articulate farewell note. Although she seems to hope that her unnamed seducer will make her a lady, she is already condemning her own wickedness and writing herself out of their lives. With a dazed look, Dan demands to know the seducer's name. Ham tells his evidence slowly, shock and suspense building higher, but at last Dan guesses the name: "Steerforth." In a burst of violence, Dan threatens to tear apart Steerforth's boat. He's especially galled by Steerforth's treachery toward his host, and wildly announces that he's going to seek out Emily.

Then, the scene ends on a curious note of grace.

Of all people, it is Mrs. Gummidge who knows
how to comfort Dan. And David, who's been feeling guilty about introducing Steerforth, finds re-
lease in tears. The novel is now halfway through,
and the plots have risen to the height of their complexity. From here on, the patterns will start working themselves out.

This might be a good time for you to draw up
your own scenario. Select several of the principal
characters and predict what might happen to them.
At the end, see how your ideas stack up against
those of Charles Dickens.

## CHAPTERS XXXII–XXXIV

Several different reactions to Emily and Steerforth are described. David finds that he admires
Steerforth's good qualities more than ever, though
he readily accepts that they must never be friends
again. (David the narrator even pauses to address
Steerforth directly, declaring that he still admires
him.) In the town, where news has traveled fast,
more people blame Emily than Steerforth—reflecting the Victorian double standard—but everyone
pities Ham and Mr. Peggotty. Mr. Peggotty announces that he will search the world for Emily.
Ham, who's staying at Yarmouth, looks dazed and
aimless, staring out to sea. Mrs. Gummidge has
become a kind, selfless woman, cheerfully helping
Dan prepare for his travels and keeping the boat-
house ready in case of Emily's return. Even volatile
Miss Mowcher shows a different side of her character. She visits David, and is stricken with remorse because she was tricked into acting as a go-
between for Steerforth and Emily. David learns he,

too, was a pawn, for Littimer had told Miss
Mowcher that David was the one pursuing Emily.
Steerforth's seduction was therefore planned long
in advance; the more you learn, the worse he looks.

---

**NOTE:**   Miss Mowcher was based on a real dwarf
who lived near Dickens. After Miss Mowcher appeared in the earlier installment, this woman wrote
to Dickens, protesting the caricature he had drawn
of her. In this chapter he makes it up to her by
showing Miss Mowcher's good side. The character
blooms into a sympathetic woman, with real feelings inside her misshapen body.

---

There is one more reaction to observe. David
takes the Peggottys to London to see Mrs. Steerforth. Proud, grand Mrs. Steerforth and homely
Mr. Peggotty appear as stark opposites in this scene,
yet each has a natural dignity. Mrs. Steerforth coldly
refuses to allow that Emily might be worthy of her
son, while Mr. Peggotty persistently tries to save
Emily from further disgrace. But once he accuses
Steerforth directly, she bursts out in anger. Beneath her words seethes pain over her son's faith-
lessness to her. And after she's stalked out of the
room, Rosa darts in, snidely accusing David of stir-
ring up trouble and pouring out a vicious diatribe
against Emily. (What do you think lies beneath her
words?) Mr. Peggotty's goodness is heightened by
his contrast to these women. As he sets out on his
search for Emily, bag over his shoulder and stick
in hand, he looks like a storybook pilgrim. With a

noble speech forgiving Emily, he walks into a glow of light.

Chapter XXXIII turns to comedy, as David describes his love for Dora. He claims he's never stopped thinking of her (though he's scarcely mentioned her for a couple of chapters). There's an ironic contrast between how grandly David talks of his love and how silly he looks, sneaking around her garden wall hoping for a glimpse of her. When he confesses his love to Peggotty, her commonsense view is refreshing. She can't understand why David is mooning around in despair, because he is a perfectly eligible suitor.

David fails to think realistically about love and marriage. When he and Peggotty see Mr. Murdstone applying for a marriage license at Mr. Spenlow's office, David remembers his mother's misery in marriage. He imagines that Murdstone's new wife will be treated the same, but he doesn't question marriage itself. He then goes into court to try a cynical divorce case. Dickens' purpose here is to make you more skeptical about marriage than the narrator David is. David's intelligent idealism may lead him to criticize the customs of the Prerogative Office (a records office of the church courts) to Mr. Spenlow's face, but he becomes an unquestioning fool as soon as he is invited to visit on Dora's birthday.

The next episode shows what a foolish lover David is, in his painfully fashionable clothes, with his extravagant gifts, riding in the dust beside Dora's carriage. Dora and he play typical lovers' games at the picnic, flirting with other people and pretending to ignore each other. But although David is gently mocking his younger self, he also makes you feel the whirl of emotions he was experiencing. After he's triumphed over his rival Red Whiskers at the picnic, he exultantly emphasizes the "I's" in a paragraph quivering with love's innocent egotism.

---

**NOTE:** Dora's new companion, Miss Mills—an "old maid" at age twenty—is Dickens' way of satirizing the popular romantic clichés of his time. Miss Mills is full of phrases like "the Desert of Sahara," "Caverns of Memory," and "a Voice from the Cloister," similar to someone quoting pop-music lyrics or TV jingles today. She's so ridiculous that David and Dora look a little less foolish, or at least a little more sincere. Love is a fad with Miss Mills. Although she helps David and Dora get together, she isn't the best guide for them.

---

When David calls on Miss Mills, she intentionally leaves him alone with Dora. In those days unmarried girls were strictly chaperoned, so this is a golden opportunity for David. In a series of passionate sentences starting with "I," he proposes to her, although this emotional outburst is not quoted directly. Little Jip barks throughout, increasing the chaos and, perhaps, emphasizing how poorly guarded Dora is. Notice that David never considers whether he ought to ask her father's permission. Why doesn't he even try? Perhaps, like Miss Mills, he simply loves the romance of a secret engagement. In a series of paragraphs starting with "When," David describes vignettes of this "insubstantial, happy, foolish time." Looking back, he can't take it seriously, but he remembers it fondly.

Notice how David's tone calms down in the next chapter when he writes to Agnes. In contrast to his dizzy emotions, the rest of his life seems stable. Peggotty keeps house for him now, and he has a good friend in Traddles, who remains cheerful in spite of his never-ending engagement and his financial losses due to Micawber. But one day, suddenly, David arrives home to find Betsey and Mr. Dick, with all their belongings, waiting for him. Mrs. Crupp's servility toward Betsey emphasizes how important a rich person is in other people's eyes, but once Mrs. Crupp leaves, Betsey explains that she has lost all her money. Calling on David to be firm and self-reliant, she faces her financial ruin with a curious mixture of grief and zest.

## CHAPTERS XXXV–XXXVII

David takes this change in fortune very seriously. He thinks he should explain to Mr. Dick what's happened, but this throws trusting Mr. Dick into such grief that David learns to keep his worries to himself. There are many small adjustments to be made. Now that Betsey has rented out her cottage, she moves in with David, while Mr. Dick sleeps in the extra bed at Peggotty's rooms. Betsey begins taking ale instead of wine for her nightly drink. She tells David that she wouldn't take the money Peggotty tried to lend them, but now she finally approves of "Barkis" (she's still prejudiced against the name Peggotty). Peggotty has told Betsey about David's love for Dora, and Betsey's hardheaded view of the situation forces David for the first time to consider whether Dora is silly (he can't actually deny it). Betsey passes a shrewd, though loving, judgment, sadly calling David "blind." That night, David mulls over his problem; now that he has no money, it'll be even harder to win Dora's hand.

---

**NOTE:** Dickens loved to describe disordered states of mind, like David's drunkenness, his lovesick frenzy, or his nightmares. He knew how the human mind worked, without the jargon of modern psychology. In this dream, Dickens jumbles together familiar figures in David's life and his underlying anxieties, all following the madcap logic of the dream-world.

---

David goes to Spenlow and asks for a refund of the money his aunt paid for him to join the office. You have to admire David's pluck in facing up to Spenlow, but Spenlow, hiding behind Jorkins' name, won't budge. David pleads with meek Mr. Jorkins himself, but he's under Spenlow's control and won't contradict him. David heads home in despair. His spirits are restored by a visit from Agnes. Though she's as serene as ever, Agnes has bad news, too: Heep is now a partner and has moved with his mother into the Wickfields' house. Heep seems to be taking over gradually, like a disease or a fungus.

Though David is depressed, Betsey is buoyant. She boldly tells off Mrs. Crupp, as David never could do. Then she explains briskly to Agnes and David how she lost her money, referring to herself in the third person, as "Betsey." She kindly assures Agnes that Mr. Wickfield had nothing to do with her bad investment. Agnes, too, lifts David's spirits. She recommends a perfect second job for David: as secretary to Dr. Strong, who has retired to London to work on his Dictionary. As she straightens up the apartment, her touch is like magic.

But then Mr. Wickfield and Uriah arrive, and David views the degeneration of Agnes' father for himself—and witnesses afresh Uriah's repulsive power. Betsey's tactless remarks to Uriah underscore his repulsiveness, yet no matter how rude she is, Uriah twists it to his advantage. Watching Agnes lovingly tending her father, David admires her more than ever. Because she's always been his confidante, he talks to her about Dora. Yet unconsciously he views Dora as a slight fairy-figure, while Agnes is a radiant source of strength. David the narrator drops an intriguing hint about what he would later know. Then, suggestively, he ends the chapter with a street beggar's unnerving echo of Betsey's words—"Blind, blind, blind!"

The next morning, David seems changed. He's taken a romantic view of his situation—that he's fighting to win Dora—and this gives him energy. He strides up to Highgate to meet with Dr. Strong, who's as absentminded as ever. Ominously, Jack Maldon is back from India, and he, too, has not changed.

---

**NOTE: Parallels** Jack is careless and callous, just like Steerforth at his worst. When Annie refuses to go out with him, her unhappiness is suspiciously similar to Emily's, and Dr. Strong's gentle concern for her is like Dan Peggotty's for his niece. David watches Jack and Annie suspiciously, now that he understands sexual treachery.

---

Traddles also comes through for David in his new situation. Traddles, of course, is used to hard work and poverty, and he can give good advice. He helps David get started learning shorthand so he can become a parliamentary reporter. He also helps Mr. Dick find work copying documents, and Dick is childishly delighted that he, too, can earn money.

Something has even turned up for Mr. Micawber, David soon learns. The Micawbers invite David and Traddles over to celebrate, but David is taken aback to hear that Micawber's new job is with Uriah Heep. David tactfully says nothing about Heep, while Mr. Micawber runs on happily, calling Uriah "my friend Heep." The Micawbers speculate that Mr. Micawber will probably become a judge, now that he's in the legal profession. Traddles tries to explain that this is impossible, the way the courts are set up, but the Micawbers ignore him, lost in their pipe dreams. Mr. Micawber makes a big show of tallying up what he owes Traddles, then proudly hands him an IOU, as if that paid the debt.

At the beginning of Chapter XXXVII, David quickly shows you how useful and practical Betsey and Peggotty have become in these new circumstances. Encouraged, David goes to the Mills' house to tell Dora about his changed prospects. But when he dramatically announces that he is now a beggar, she can't understand what he means, and weeps with fright. David pours out a stream of romantic statements, but she still doesn't absorb what he's telling her. She agrees to be poor with him, then insists that Jip must have his mutton chop every day. David admits to himself that he's a little disappointed in Dora. Though he's charmed by her childishness, he tries to suggest that she learn some cooking and housekeeping, only to trigger another flood of tears. Even Miss Mills, with her clichés about the "Cottage of content," comprehends David's news better than Dora does. But with surprising insight, she also warns David not to expect Dora ever to become domestic.

---

**NOTE:** By this time, David is too much in love to help himself, and Dora's shallowness torments him. Her agitation, too, seems genuine. Sheltered and spoiled, she simply cannot understand David's position, but she does want to understand. She must care for him because she's so frightened by anything that might destroy their love. How has the narrator's tone of voice changed? (Compare it to the earlier passages about Dora.) What is the significance of this change?

---

David's old fairy-tale images go out of control; he sees himself as the "Monster" in Dora's "Fairy's bower." (What deeper psychological or sexual meaning might this image of the invading monster have?) David is still fascinated by her singing and chatter, but now that he has taken a serious attitude toward the rest of his life, he begins to see how inadequate his romantic vision of love is. He ends this installment as he began it, worrying.

# CHAPTERS XXXVIII–XL

As David describes his efforts to learn short-hand, you get a typically Dickensian flight of fancy: the dots, circles, and curves seem to come to life, turning into flies, cobwebs, and skyrockets, maliciously haunting David. To give David practice, Betsey, Mr. Dick, and Traddles play Parliament in David's rooms at night. This scene is a satiric parody of the real Parliament, but what else does it show about these personalities? Would you enjoy being part of this circle of friends?

In contrast to their lively play-acting, David is soon confronted by self-important Mr. Spenlow and cold Miss Murdstone. Miss Murdstone produces David's love letters, which she discovered (thanks to Jip). Though she pretends to be doing her duty, she's also getting revenge on David. Once more she fills the role of the fairy-tale dragon in David's life. Manfully, he admits he was wrong to court Dora secretly, but says he won't stop loving her. Note the indirect quotes of his emotional replies.

---

**NOTE: Parallels**  Like Mrs. Steerforth, Mr. Spenlow speaks coldly about how his plans for his daughter do not include David. He accuses David of abusing his hospitality, just as Dan Peggotty accused Steerforth, but without Dan's simple emotion. Is David the seducer or the victim here? Mr. Spenlow's mercenary talk about Dora's inheritance is quite different from Mr. Wickfield's doting on Agnes, but both fathers seem to live for their daughters.

---

Afterwards, David writes a wild letter to Mr. Spenlow and a desperate note to Miss Mills, but his emotional reaction is a relief in a world of heartless Spenlows and Murdstones. Just then, however, fate does a strange turn. Arriving at the office next morning, David learns that Mr. Spenlow died of a fit on his way home last night. By inventing this plot twist, Dickens may have conveniently gotten Dora's father out of the way, but he makes the sudden death effective. David's mind whirls with conflicting emotions. Most of his grief is selfish—he even feels jealous of death. He sends a note of condolence to Dora, but it's really a bid for her attention.

Ironically, Mr. Spenlow, for all his talk about Dora's inheritance, hasn't even left a will. David is surprised, but Mr. Jorkins and the clerk, Mr. Tiffey, have seen more of the world and know how often men lie about their wills. Spenlow's hypocrisy is revealed even further. In spite of his businesslike airs, he couldn't handle his own affairs, and he died in debt. Penniless Dora must go to live with two maiden aunts. David's only contact with her for a while is through Miss Mills' diary, which she lends him. Underneath the clichés and the coy initials Julia uses instead of names, this diary shows Dora grieving weakly, doting on Jip, and feeling guilty for her father's death. She's not nearly ready to reconcile with David, and he uses fairy-tale imagery again to describe his hopeless case.

After a satirical passage on the shadier aspects of the Commons, David willingly leaves London to handle some business in Dover for his aunt. Stopping in Canterbury to visit the Wickfields, he sees Mr. Micawber at work, and notes his uneasy, secretive manner. Curiously, Micawber makes a suggestive remark about David and Agnes, and David feels a weird shiver of déjà vu. This should alert you to the undercurrents of meaning in the conversation that follows. As David tells Agnes how he depends upon her good influence, she remains oddly silent. She firmly reminds him that he should depend on Dora, and she gives him good advice about how to woo Dora. How do you think Agnes is feeling here?

---

**NOTE: Metaphor**  In Dickens' world, people and objects are vitally connected. Notice how this house expresses relationships. Heep's office is a new, raw addition. Mr. Wickfield's office is "a shadow of its former self," many of its furnishings removed by Heep. Uriah has taken David's old bedroom, just as he hopes to take David's place in Agnes' heart.

---

The Heeps hover over the Wickfields, never leaving them alone, like jailors guarding their prisoners. (David compares them to bats.) Uriah even follows David on his evening walk. When David tries to get rid of him, Uriah coolly explains that he must watch David, as his rival for Agnes. David sounds stiff and pompous—"I am engaged to another young lady," he explains. But Heep is maddening; he refuses to let David hurt his feelings, and yet he subtly accuses and mocks David. Goaded, David insults Uriah openly. Then Uriah tells David the pathetic story of his upbringing in a charity school. How does this make you feel about Heep? Why do you think Dickens put this in here?

At dinner, when Heep tricks Mr. Wickfield into drinking too much and torments him by proposing a toast to Agnes, Heep is too horrible for sympathy. He's pushed too far, and Mr. Wickfield flies into an incoherent rage. (Notice that David quiets Mr. Wickfield by reminding him of the connection between David and Agnes. What do you make of this?) In a dramatic dialogue, Wickfield eloquently denounces Heep, and describes with sorrow how his absorption first in his wife, then in Agnes, diseased his mind. Heep seems flustered, but isn't human enough to feel Mr. Wickfield's pain. David later begs Agnes not to throw herself away to please her father. Her startled reaction again suggests deeper feelings for David. Back in London, when David tells Betsey this, she ponders it gravely. Perhaps she, too, wonders what really lies between David and Agnes.

The mood changes to melodrama as, on a snowy night, David sees Dan Peggotty on the steps of a church. Carrying a little burden, he looks like a mythical figure of the Wanderer, with long, gray hair and a sun-beaten, wrinkled face. Mysteriously, Martha Endell flits through the same snowstorm. She listens outside the door of the inn as Dan tells David of his travels. Dan's simple dialect and emotions make him an effective narrator. Though he's modest about his skills, Dan has been a great detective. Doggedly he followed Emily's trail across Europe, and he came close to finding her at one point. He paints a sentimental picture of the European villagers who helped him along the way. And as he speaks of his forgiveness for Emily, Martha listens intently.

**NOTE: Emily's sin**   Dan is so forgiving and the people he meets are so helpful that modern readers sometimes lose sight of the severity of Emily's sin by Victorian standards. (Notice how Martha has been cast out; in this scene, she's literally "out in the cold.") Though Emily is living like a lady with Steerforth, it's assumed that he'll never marry her and will eventually abandon her. You may say that she must have loved Steerforth to go off with him, but in Dickens' time that was no excuse. Her letter is full of shame and sorrow, and never speaks of love for Steerforth. Dickens must show that she's repentant and not a creature of lust, because his original readers would have been so scandalized by her behavior.

# CHAPTERS XLI–XLIII

David doesn't seem like such a ridiculous young lover anymore. As he receives an answer to his letter to Dora's aunts, his narrative tone is slightly satiric, but steady. Love still makes him egocentric; when he learns that Mr. Mills is moving to India, David reacts as though it were done only to foil him. But Miss Mills' leaving does seem to signal the end of his clandestine, romantic courtship, and the beginning of a more normal one.

Traddles now looks like the comic suitor, in contrast to David. As the two young men walk to Putney to visit the aunts, David shows you for the first time how Traddles' hair sticks straight up. Traddles' story about his proposal to Sophy is comical, but it's also a warning that families can make things difficult for young lovers.

At the aunts' house, David is so nervous that everything seems exaggerated, fragmented, as in a dream. The aunts look like Mr. Spenlow, but they are birdlike and harmless. As they talk, they chime in on each other's words, just as the Murdstones did, but their formal speeches are like prim little chirps. Miss Lavinia, who was "disappointed in love," is like an elderly version of Miss Mills—silly but sympathetic. Miss Clarissa, her arms crossed, is still brooding over how they were slighted by Dora's parents. Both have led unfulfilled lives, and they're excited to have something interesting happening at last. At what point do you think they decide to accept David? When you hear Jip's stifled bark on the other side of the door, you know that Dora is listening. Once David has agreed to their terms (which are really quite easy), he's led to Dora, who's comically hiding in the next room.

Still, there are some unsettling details. Dora's fear of Traddles and of Betsey's promised visits shows her spoiled, timid nature. Jip's howls whenever Aunt Betsey visits ruffle the otherwise smooth relations of the two families. David notices that all three aunts treat Dora like a little doll, and she seems to like it. When he points this out to her, the criticism makes her cry. On the other hand, Dora tries to learn cooking and household accounts for David's sake, though she simply can't manage it and the cookbook becomes a perch for Jip. Dora fits her new nickname, Little Blossom, and even David can't help treating her like a toy sometimes. How does his new nickname, Doady, seem to suit him? What image of him does it create?

In the beginning of the next chapter, David speaks in a serious, honest voice about how hard work,

concentration, and discipline have been the secret
of his success. This is the older narrator David
speaking, and perhaps it's straight from Dickens'
heart, too. David is becoming a responsible young
man now, and this side of him naturally surfaces
when Agnes appears. The Wickfields (accom-
panied by the Heeps, of course) are in town to visit
the Strongs, and David must endure Uriah and his
vicious talk about the Strongs.

---

**NOTE:**   David has had suspicions of Annie and
Jack, too, but Uriah's are more selfish and mean.
Uriah is jealous of Annie's friendship with Agnes,
and resents Jack's superior airs, so he spitefully
determines to bring them down. You still have no
hard evidence of any affair, but Dickens is deliberately leaving ambiguous clues. What is David's
reaction to these bits of information? Is there any
evidence to show what is going on with Annie at
this point?

---

When Agnes meets Dora, Dora at first acts silly
and scared, but Agnes' kind nature wins her over.
Both come off well in this scene. While Agnes is
typically serene and good, Dora is radiantly pretty
and affectionate. Dora even becomes thoughtful,
confessing to David that she feels inadequate compared to Agnes, and wondering why he fell in love
with her (instead of with Agnes, she implies). David
and Dora both grow more serious, as does their
love.

As David sees Agnes home, she assures him that
she'll never accept Uriah. Immediately thereafter,
David stops by Dr. Strong's study and views a

scene, posed like a still photograph, of Uriah tormenting Dr. Strong, and Mr. Wickfield watching helplessly. The scene then comes to life: Uriah is telling Dr. Strong his suspicions about Annie and Jack. Like a horrible master of ceremonies, Uriah spins out his evidence, and he drags David and Mr. Wickfield into admitting their misgivings, too, making everyone miserable. But Dr. Strong responds differently than Uriah expected. (Is Uriah too inhuman to predict people's reactions?) Blaming himself for putting Annie in an unhappy position, Dr. Strong gallantly vows to bear his knowledge in silence. David admires his simple chivalry, but Heep is furious that he can't cause the trouble he hoped to. Left alone with Heep, David loses his temper and strikes Uriah on the cheek. Uriah even turns that against David, saying he always liked David and forgiving him. This makes David feel guilty, but he doesn't apologize, and he remains openly hateful of Uriah.

David recounts gently, sorrowfully, the change that comes over the Strongs in the next few weeks. Ironically, the only person who can comfort them is Mr. Dick, with his simple goodness. In a letter from Mrs. Micawber, David learns that Mr. Micawber has become secretive and depressed. Even this happy home has been attacked by Heep's bad influence.

This installment ends with another chapter of present-tense retrospect.

---

**NOTE: Cinematic technique** The major characters appear here in silent scenes, almost like a film montage, showing snatches of life that tell their story. You hear a few words of dialogue at peak moments, but the rest is visual. Dickens provides settings and costumes with careful detail. At the wedding, "extras" are used to fill the crowd.

---

David courts Dora throughout the seasons of the year. He spends hours in Parliament, scribbling down the debates. He writes stories that appear in magazines. David moves to a cottage in the suburbs, and he and Dora shop for furniture (though they buy only a ridiculous house for Jip). Peggotty comes to clean up; Mr. Peggotty glides by in the streets at night. Everyone finally gathers for David and Dora's wedding, which he views like a sleepwalker. It's lovely and comic, but at the end Dora asks him in her most childish voice, "Are you happy now, you foolish boy? and sure you don't repent?" How does this make you feel about their marriage?

## CHAPTERS XLIV–XLVI

Being married is strange for David. Now that the courtship is over, he doesn't quite know what to do with Dora.

---

**NOTE:** Dora's always seemed like a child or a doll, not a woman. David's courtship has been full of romantic images, rather than physical desire. You've seen him kiss Dora's "rosebud" mouth only a couple of times. In Victorian society, girls were often sheltered from sex (and Dora hasn't even had a mother to tell her the facts of life). Dickens is never explicit about sex, but part of David's uncertainty may arise from the awkwardness of their new physical relationship.

---

David may not deal with the reality of sex, but he does talk about the reality of housekeeping, which is equally revealing. Their servant Mary Anne is dishonest and incompetent, and that's the cause of their first quarrel. (Ominously, this is the first scene you see dramatized from their marriage.) Dora is hurt by David's criticism of her housekeeping, and accuses him of being mean. Some readers think Dora is being silly and David is weak not to scold her more. Others think David is being unfair to Dora, and he should know her better. That's the attitude Betsey takes when she stops by that night. Betsey has grown kinder and gentler. She says loving things about Dora, and she is tactful as she points out to David the realities of his marriage. She also wisely refuses to interfere.

David and Dora soon make up, but the housekeeping doesn't improve. They seem to have no control over the situation: servants, stores, even cookbooks automatically sabotage them. David describes the disorder in a dry but helpless tone of voice. Household objects seem to have a life of their own. Though Dora serves a badly cooked meal when Traddles comes to dinner, David is still too enchanted by her to scold her. That night, Dora asks David to give her a new name—"child-wife"—trying to explain that he shouldn't blame her for being herself.

Dora struggles over the household books, never making any progress, while David writes his sto-

ries at night. The narrative tone is teasing but loving. Following Dr. Strong's example, David admits
that he keeps his worries to himself rather than
sharing them with his wife, and that he sometimes
misses his romantic ideals. But he's also touched
by Dora's pleasure in waiting up for him, holding
his pens as he writes, or carrying useless keys in
a basket similar to Agnes'. Dora's affectionate nature helps him overlook her faults.

David turns his attention to the Strongs' unhappy situation. Unlike Betsey, Mrs. Markleham
interferes destructively in the Strongs' marriage.
But Mr. Dick announces that because he's such a
simpleton he alone can heal the rift between Dr.
Strong and Annie. The rest of this chapter reveals
Mr. Dick's plan. David and Betsey visit the Strongs
one day. (Though they won't be active partici-
pants, Dickens needs to have them witness this
scene.) It's a melancholy setting—an autumn twi-
light, with a smell of dead leaves that reminds David
of his childhood.

Mrs. Markleham bursts into the parlor to announce to Annie and her guests that she's just
overheard Dr. Strong tell his lawyers to draw up
a will, leaving everything to Annie. They all go to
the study, where Dr. Strong is sitting calmly at his
desk. Like an unobtrusive stage manager, Mr. Dick
leads Annie to her husband. She's so moved by
what he's done that she kneels at his feet. David
is called on to repeat Uriah's accusations. Then,
for the first time, you learn Annie's side of the
story. Her confession is grave, eloquent, and emotional. To keep it from being too sentimental, Dickens presents it along with Mrs. Markleham's of-
fended cries, Betsey's wry retorts, and Dr. Strong's

gentle protests. Annie says she's always loved Dr.
Strong, and in spite of her mother's meddling she
never gave herself to Jack Maldon. She recognized
Jack's deceitful nature the night he stole the ribbon
from her dress, but she never told the Doctor for
fear of hurting him. Once the reconciliation is complete, the guests steal away, leaving husband and
wife tenderly together.

---

**NOTE: Annie's words**  David is struck deeply by
a few phrases of Annie's, which he remembers
long afterwards. She says her love for Jack Maldon
is "the first mistaken impulse of an undisciplined
heart." David doesn't say why this affects him, but
you may guess that he's thinking of Dora, and of
the "unsuitability of mind and purpose" of his
marriage. In contrast, Annie's love for Dr. Strong
is "founded on a rock." Do you think David already longs for a stronger foundation for his love?
Is this feeling conscious or unconscious?

---

This installment contains domestic comedy,
melodrama, and now Gothic romance. Passing the
Steerforths' house one night, noticing its dead look,
David is called in to see Rosa. Here again he establishes a mood with the setting: the landscape is
"lurid," "scowling," and has a "sullen glare," all
of which also defines Rosa. Her features seem exaggerated, especially the scar, and her darting
speech has become fierce and imperious. David
compares her to a vengeful fairy-tale princess. Littimer, like her evil gnome, tells David the story of
Steerforth abandoning Emily.

**NOTE: Emily's character**    Dickens is still making Emily look as good as possible. You learn that she cut a fine figure in Europe, and even Steerforth was so impressed that he stayed with her longer than he expected to. In fact, Emily's own guilt and regret soured the relationship. Often depressed, she made friends with boatmen's families everywhere, as though longing for her home. She raged when Steerforth left her, but she had enough integrity to run away rather than marry Littimer, as Steerforth had callously proposed.

In contrast to Rosa, Mrs. Steerforth, who finds them talking, is dignified by her sorrow. Like Rosa, however, she thinks Emily is a mercenary girl who may still threaten James. David defends Emily, and afterwards goes immediately to Mr. Peggotty to give him the news. Dan is, in his own way, as dignified as Mrs. Steerforth. Yet he's more forgiving and open-minded than she is. He agrees with David that they should ask Martha Endell to help them find Emily.

## CHAPTERS XLVII–L

Dickens loved to walk the streets of London at night, and he recreates them vividly here, as David and Mr. Peggotty follow Martha. Finally, on a dark side street in a nightmarish neighborhood, Martha halts on the riverbank as though she's about to throw herself in. David grabs her arm and stops her, but she seems haunted by the river, babbling that it's the only place for her.

---

**NOTE: Drowning**   Martha consciously compares
herself to the river, which begins pure in the country and ends polluted in the great troubled sea.
Ham and Emily also are drawn to water, and the
image of drowning is connected with all three of
them. Drowning may also be a metaphor for emotional and sexual desire, which brings grief to these
characters.

---

In the dark, following this brush with death, the
melodrama continues. Notice how eloquent Martha's speech is (she doesn't use dialect). She reminds you of Emily's goodness and then describes
the wretched life of a disgraced woman, pointing
out to Mr. Peggotty that even he has spurned her.
In contrast, in simple dialect he says he's changed
his views, that he loves Emily and needs Martha's
aid. She dramatically vows to help, but refuses to
take any money, saying that the trust they put in
her may save her soul.

Another mystery meets David when he gets
home. The shabby, sullen stranger is in Aunt Betsey's garden, and David sees her give the man
some money. He accepts it ungratefully, whining
for more; Betsey cries out that he has hurt her
enough already. After he leaves, David approaches her and begs to know the truth about this
man. She confesses that it's her husband, who's
not dead, as everyone thought.

---

**NOTE:**   Speaking of herself in the third person,
Betsey tells David how much she once loved this

man. If you're surprised to hear that she was once so romantic, note that she says she buried her feelings after he hurt her. Think back and see how this explains her behavior toward many people, including David's parents.

---

In the next chapter, David's own marriage is examined. He modestly describes the success of his first novel, and how that made life easier. His worldly success, however, contrasts with the disorder in his home. The arrest of their page shows how badly David and Dora are victimized, not only by their servants but also by all the local tradesmen. No longer does David blame outside sources; he tells Dora they are at fault for not being better managers. Dora reacts defensively, as she did when he criticized her before, but her sobbing isn't so effective now. He simply decides to take another tack with her.

---

**NOTE:**  Some readers have felt that David is acting like Mr. Murdstone in teaching his wife new habits, and that Dickens disapproves. Others think Dickens is merely mocking David for trying to change a child like Dora. David's speeches to Dora do sound a little self-righteous, but they are standard Victorian rhetoric about social duty and domestic order. Dickens portrays David's efforts to teach Dora with irony, but it's hard to tell whether David or Dora is the object of satire. (It may be both!)

---

Oddly enough, Dora keeps questioning their

marriage. She knows what David has been trying to do, and when he confesses it, she suggests—not for the first time—that he shouldn't have married her. She begins a question: "Are you sure you don't think, sometimes, it would have been better to have—" Some readers think she's about to say how much better a wife Agnes would be, but David doesn't pick up on it. He isn't as insightful as Dora is. He feels melancholy, and though he knows it's normal for youthful fancies to fade, he senses that his marriage lacks something that other marriages have. (This leads him to think of Agnes, you notice.) But he can't imagine life without Dora, and, in straightforward sentences he describes how he loves her. Rather than admit he's made a mistake, he tries to discipline his "undisciplined heart." Feeling guilty for being unhappy, he struggles to content himself with Dora.

By now the situation is gently tragic. Dora becomes pregnant, and David hopes motherhood will mature her, but the baby dies. Notice the sentimental language, typically Victorian in its euphemisms about pregnancy and childbirth. Dora never fully recovers, and as she notices that Jip is getting old, a sense of mortality begins to settle on her. She is sweeter and more affectionate than ever, but David reflects ruefully on another meaning of her nickname "Little Blossom," that like a flower she must wither and die.

Another mystery brews in Chapter XLIX. David receives a letter from Mr. Micawber which is so wordy and convoluted that David can hardly understand any of it, except that Micawber is in trouble and wants to talk. Traddles arrives with a similar letter from Mrs. Micawber, begging for help with the change in her husband. Intrigued, Traddles and David go to meet Mr. Micawber. He seems downcast and uneasy and responds bitterly to David's inquiries about Heep. Although he speaks in his characteristic style, he's dejected. How does this affect the comedy here? They take him to Betsey's cottage to cheer him up, but Micawber has a hard time even making punch. The rest of the party watches him restlessly. Finally Micawber breaks down and explodes into an agitated, broken speech about the fraud and hypocrisy he has witnessed. The hated name "HEEP" rises during this speech like a violent hiccup. Finally Micawber rushes out, but he sends a coherent letter from a nearby tavern, politely inviting them all to Canterbury next week where, he promises intriguingly, he will perform his "duty."

The very next night another mystery rises to a climax. On a still evening after a heavy rain (symbolic weather), Martha arrives at David's cottage and, without an explanation, leads him to town. Their destination is a dilapidated, crowded lodging house. A figure flits up the rotten stairs ahead of them, and with amazement David recognizes Rosa Dartle. Martha leads David into a small room adjoining the room Rosa went into. Through the door, David can hear Rosa's showdown with Emily. You have to follow this scene by sounds only, like a radio play. David is merely a convenient observer; he can't interfere until Mr. Peggotty arrives.

The scene between the women is wrenching and melodramatic. Rosa insults and accuses Emily, who protests with tears and anguish. Rosa has been transformed completely into a villainess, while

Emily is sweet and repentant. When Emily speaks of how she loved Steerforth, Rosa explodes, "You love him?"—suggesting that her own frustrated love has fed this rage. Mocking Emily's honesty, Rosa warns her to hide herself, then steps dramatically from the room. A second later Dan Peggotty rushes in to catch his distraught niece as she faints.

## CHAPTERS LI–LII

Mr. Peggotty comes to David's house the next day to tell Emily's story. Like her uncle, Emily made friends with local people in Europe. After she ran away from Littimer, a village woman took her in and nursed her through a fever. Next Emily went to France, where she worked as a waitress. When Littimer came to the inn, Emily ran away again, to London. There a woman befriended her and offered her work. Dickens isn't explicit, but the work was probably prostitution. Martha saved Emily just in time.

---

**NOTE: Allusions**   Just as Micawber frequently quotes Shakespeare or poetry, Mr. Peggotty quotes the Bible because it's so familiar to him. For example, he says the good deeds of the people who helped Emily are "laid up wheer neither moth nor rust doth corrupt, and wheer thieves do not break through nor steal" (Matthew 6:19–20). Emily's story also parallels Bible stories. Like Eve, she's been cast out of a happy home for her sins; Littimer is described as the snake who led her into it. Also, the pregnant woman who befriends Emily appears like the Blessed Mother.

---

Mr. Peggotty announces that he and Emily will emigrate to Australia to begin a new life. He discusses his arrangements for Ham, Peggotty, and Mrs. Gummidge, who'll remain in England. Then he pulls out all the money Emily had from Steerforth, and asks David to return it to Mrs. Steerforth. What is the effect of this gesture?

David accompanies Mr. Peggotty to Yarmouth. His visit to Mr. Omer provides comic relief, as the old man rattles on about his age and infirmity (this also gives you a sense that time has passed). Omer praises David for his novel, though David, mocking himself, makes it clear that Omer fell asleep over it. But Omer is glad to hear of Emily's return and Martha's good deed. Do you think this means that the community has forgiven them? Why?

As David visits with the Peggotty family, they seem as loving as ever, but a shadow lies over them, especially Ham. Ham tells David that he blames himself for pressing his affections on Emily (as Dr. Strong did with Annie). He asks David to tell Emily that he isn't greatly hurt, so she won't worry, but it's clear he still loves her and finds no purpose in life without her. As the old boat-house is being shut up, Mrs. Gummidge suddenly pleads with Dan not to leave her behind. The good in both of them is called out at the moment of parting, and he decides to take her to Australia.

Though Dora is ill, she insists that David leave her again a few days later for his appointment with Mr. Micawber. This allows Dickens to juggle several plots without David seeming to ignore his dying wife. It also reminds you of how unselfish Dora is. David, Betsey, Mr. Dick, and Traddles head for Canterbury.

---

**NOTE:** Dickens seems to love Canterbury specially, he describes it so often. Almost every time David comes here, he strolls around and describes how old and peaceful it seems. This time, the bells also warn him of Dora's death. David's romantic nature emerges in these solitary, nostalgic walks.

---

Waiting for Micawber at the inn, each character shows his or her nature in a different kind of restless behavior. Comedy is often a matter of stripping off masks, and many people's true natures are revealed in this chapter. When Micawber arrives, for example, David learns that dull, plodding Traddles has cleverly assisted Micawber in his scheme. When they go to Wickfield & Heep's, Micawber appears to work hard, but the huge ruler stuck inside his vest reveals his true intentions. When they walk into Heep's office, David glimpses Heep's mean face before the mask of humble hypocrisy takes over. But Agnes' beauty shines through her anxiety.

Micawber begins the confrontation by refusing to leave when Heep orders him to. Heep's face first turns pale, then darkens (later in the scene it turns blue!) as Micawber calls him a scoundrel. Heep turns on his old rival David, accusing him of being behind all this. Uriah is always motivated by personal resentment, so he assumes others are, too. Like a cornered animal, he lashes out, threatening everyone, even calling Mr. Wickfield an "old ass."

In high comic style, Micawber formally accuses

Heep by reading aloud a verbose letter, while
brandishing his ruler like a sword. He explains that
Heep gained power over him by lending him
money, but that he stayed on only to gather evidence against Heep. He has discovered that Heep
falsified business deals, tricked Mr. Wickfield into
signing over control of the firm's money, forged
Wickfield's signature, and framed him for embez-
zlement. Heep swindled Mr. Wickfield into signing over to him the entire partnership and even
his house. Micawber has evidence, too: a half-
burned notebook Mrs. Micawber found in the fire-
place of the Heeps' old house. After he concludes
this elaborate letter, Betsey grabs Uriah and bluntly
demands her money back. She now admits that
she thought Mr. Wickfield had lost her money,
though she kept silent for Agnes' sake.

Mrs. Heep cringes and whines during all this.
At least Uriah faces it with a vicious courage. When
Traddles offers to call in the police if Uriah doesn't
hand over the rest of the documents, however,
Uriah caves in like a coward. Yet when David
preaches to Uriah about greed and cunning, Uriah
snaps back at him, unrepentant.

The party then moves to the Micawbers' house,
where Mr. and Mrs. Micawber are reconciled. Typically, Mr. Micawber embraces poverty one moment, then jumps at Betsey's suggestion that they
emigrate, as though it had been his lifelong dream.
Of course, he asks her for a loan to carry it out.

---

**NOTE:**   The Micawbers are the second group that
heads for Australia to start afresh. Emigration to
Australia was very popular in the 1840s, shortly

before Dickens wrote this novel. It was considered a land of second chances, so Dickens' readers would have been hopeful for Micawber's success. Do you find this believable?

---

Comedy is swiftly replaced by David's sad account of Dora's death. It's another present-tense retrospect, highlighted scenes presented simply through dialogue, as David sits numbly at Dora's bedside. Dora is idealized, seeming sweet, gentle, and wise. In each scene she moves farther from this world. She begins by remembering the past fondly. In the next vignette she prepares her mind for death. In the third, she speaks of herself in the past tense, and imagines the unhappy future she and David would have had. Why do you think Dickens has Agnes, not David, with Dora when she dies? Is it fitting? Dickens keeps death offstage for dramatic effect. Alone downstairs, David broods over his regrets for their marriage. Then, with a final whine, loyal old Jip dies at the same moment as Dora. Agnes appears like an angel, pointing upward to Dora but also to heaven. Then grief overcomes David.

## CHAPTERS LIV–LVII

David begins this installment by telling of his sorrow and describing Agnes' saintly support in his grief.

---

**NOTE:**   Many of Dickens' first readers would have begun this chapter a couple of weeks after they'd read about Dora's death. Notice how Dickens skillfully reminds them of what happened last month and re-establishes his mood.

Then he plunges back into comedy, as the Micawbers make a big show of preparing themselves for Australia. At this stage, Dickens has to tie up many threads of his plot, and he does so quickly. Traddles tells David that Mr. Wickfield's affairs have been settled, though Agnes has decided he should retire while she supports them by keeping a school. As Traddles reports that Betsey's money has been recovered, she surprisingly reveals that she had 2000 pounds left all the time, but she kept it a secret to test David's self-reliance. Heep, nasty to the end, appears to have left town with his mother. Traddles' shrewd summary of Heep's character shows Dickens' insight into human psychology. Micawber's affairs, you learn, are comically tangled, since he still owes several debts. Magnanimously, Betsey intends to give him a lump sum to pay them off, but David and Traddles know Micawber better. They work out a way to pay his debts and give him capital for his new life, without having to trust him with cash. Only moments later, they have to save Micawber from being arrested.

One sad affair must be settled. Traddles reminds Betsey that Heep threatened to hurt her through her husband. This danger fades forever as Betsey and David attend the poor man's funeral. The chapter ends on a note of comedy as Micawber writes in despair, announcing another arrest for debt, only to add in a P.S. that Traddles has just paid it off.

The mood changes swiftly to suspense in the next chapter. David prepares you for an event so awful, it still haunts him. Learning from Peggotty of Ham's strength in his sorrow, David decides to write to Emily, telling her of Ham's forgiveness, so she can respond before she sails for Australia. Emily sends back to David a grateful note to Ham, and David decides to take it to Ham. On his way down, however, he meets a violent storm.

---

**NOTE:** This storm seems unnatural and chaotic, like the end of the world. It comes from the sea, which is associated in this book with life and death. What does the storm stand for? Some readers think it symbolizes fate, as it relentlessly advances and carelessly batters people around. Others think it represents Dickens' view that life is dark, violent, and confusing.

---

Ominously, Ham isn't home when David gets to Yarmouth, and David feels uneasy at the inn when he hears stories of foundered ships offshore. He sleeps fitfully that night. Next morning, he's awakened by news that a ship has been wrecked on the beach, and he runs to join the crowd watching it. One figure in a red cap stands out among the struggling survivors on deck. The roaring of the wind and waves almost create a silence. The only sound is the ship's bell, tolling its death knell. Then David sees Ham volunteer to wade out to save the men. The way Ham looks out to sea convinces David that he wants to die. David tries to stop him, as he once stopped Martha from suicide.

Ham's cheerful, resigned voice rings through the confusion, begging David to let him go.

The action is set up almost like fast-cutting camera shots. Now you see the lone figure clinging to the mast, waving his red cap (David is reminded strangely of Steerforth). Now you see Ham plunging forward, flung about by the waves. The men haul in the rope, and Ham lies on shore, dead. The body is taken to a nearby cottage. Then David is called away by a kind old fisherman, who leads him to the beach to view the corpse of the shipwreck's victim—Steerforth.

---

**NOTE:**   Dickens packs this final shot with life's grim ironies. This beach is where Emily once played innocently. The boat-house stood nearby, but it's been wrecked by the storm, just as its family was wrecked by tragedy. In death, Steerforth is handsome, graceful, boyish again. The cruelest irony is that Ham died trying to save the man who destroyed his reason for living.

---

David accompanies Steerforth's corpse back to London. It's an autumn day, but bright and peaceful after the storm. David goes to Steerforth's house, where invalid Mrs. Steerforth sits in her beloved son's room, surviving on her memories of him. David tries to break his news gently, but Rosa picks up the truth. In the end, she's the one who tells Mrs. Steerforth, harshly, tauntingly. Rosa accuses the old woman of ruining her son and bitterly describes how she herself once loved him with selfless devotion, only to be discarded. Rosa works herself up to a mad pitch, and David urges her to be kinder to the old woman in her grief. But Mrs. Steerforth never says a word, sitting rigid in her chair, moaning dully. Suddenly, Rosa realizes the woman's had a stroke, and frantically tries to care for her. How do you account for her behavior here?

David decides to keep the tragic news from the emigrants, with Mr. Micawber's help, until they have safely sailed. Comically, the entire Micawber family is dressed in seafaring clothes the night before they set off. In a tumble-down lodging house, Micawber brews his famous punch with his old zest, but he makes his family drink out of sailors' tin mugs. One more time he is arrested and bailed out; one more time he hands Traddles an IOU. One more time Mrs. Micawber predicts that her family will come around and that her husband's talents will be recognized.

Peggotty and David go on board the next day to see the passengers off. (Micawber's been arrested once more in the interim.) David sketches, as a journalist might, the scene below deck: dark, cramped, cluttered, with a wide spectrum of society thrown together, cheerfully looking to their future. He sees Emily through the crowd, and even thinks he sees Agnes, like an angel of mercy, bidding her good-bye.

---

**NOTE: Emily's distance**  Ever since Emily returned to London, she's been kept offstage. David hears her through a door, learns her story from her uncle, and reads her letter, but never meets her face to face. Dickens thus pulls off several effects: he accentuates her shame, as though she's hiding; he keeps her at a distance, as an idealized tragic figure; and he avoids having to show how her sexual experience has changed her. After all, good as her heart is, she is still a fallen woman, and Dickens would have had to show that.

At the last moment, David learns that generous Mr. Peggotty is also taking Martha with him to start a new life. As David and Peggotty return to shore, the boat leaves, amid cheers, in a blaze of sunset, and David finally catches a glimpse of Emily beside her uncle. The scene is hopeful and uplifting, but David's own grief begins to settle on him as dusk falls.

## CHAPTERS LVIII–LXIV

Most of the plots in this complex novel have now had their climaxes. The final double installment rounds off the book. It begins with a transitional chapter, as David leaves for the Continent to work through his grief. He's shattered, numb. If David's mourning seems excessive to you, remember that the Victorians were very sentimental about death and loss. Remember also that you should see David as a sensitive artist, who's grieving not only for his wife but for his best friend. He wanders throughout Europe, but unlike Mr. Peggotty, his wandering has no purpose; he scarcely notices anything. He's convinced he'll never get over his sadness.

But one evening in Switzerland, the view of a beautiful valley somehow opens his heart again. (The Victorians were great believers in the healing powers of nature.) He hears a distant singing that could almost be from heaven. Then he receives a letter from his guardian angel—Agnes—who says exactly what he needs to hear about surviving his sorrow. He is revived by human contact (like Emily and Dan Peggotty, he makes friends with local people) and, more importantly, by his own work. The discipline of hard work strengthens him. Also, though he doesn't make a big point of it, turning his experiences into fiction eases his heart.

Gradually he begins to realize that he has always loved Agnes. But grief has changed David from the bright young lover who won Dora's hand, and he pessimistically tells himself he's lost his chance with Agnes. He's sure she feels merely a sister's love for him, and that it's his fault. Though he suspects she once felt something more, he assumes that his boyish passions persuaded her to change her attitude. Feeling it wouldn't be fair to go to Agnes now, he stays away from England until three years have passed. Do you think David is aware of his true feelings here? If not, what feelings is he denying—and why?

Because David has changed, England looks different to him when he returns. London is dark and dirty. The waiters at the inn are old and solemn (compare them to the sly, talkative waiters David met in his youth). The inn itself is old, stodgy, and mired in the past. On his way to visit Traddles, David feels pessimistic about his friend's chances of success in such a society. Traddles is still cheerful and loyal, but a change has come into his life, too. He's finally married to Sophy. The tiny apartment is crowded with her and her sisters living there, but unlike Dora, Sophy appears to be a great manager. Traddles acts cautious of David's feelings. Although David claims to be joyful for them, he does seem a little detached, merely sitting and listening to them. Traddles' understated account of his absurd courtship is comical, though a bit pathetic. Watching them, David admires Sophy's domestic virtues. He's critical of her sisters and the way they let themselves be waited on, but their love and liveliness turns his criticism to approval. What does this tell you about what David wants out of life? Notice that once again he thinks of Agnes, though he resigns himself to having lost her.

Since David is a new man, it's appropriate that he runs into Dr. Chillip, who brought him into the world. David's childhood is replayed in their conversation, although meek little Chillip is really more interested in David's present fame as a writer (another reminder of how David has changed). Chillip tells David about the Murdstones' tyranny over a new young wife.

David revives another period of his life by heading to Dover to his aunt's. Betsey updates David on all his old friends, who are thriving. Their dialogue is dramatized when it comes to the most important old friend, Agnes. Betsey doesn't say so, but the way she looks at David and praises Agnes suggests that she feels there's something between them. David, however, is too full of nostalgic thoughts to notice this. He asks if Agnes has any lovers, and Betsey cryptically tells him that she suspects Agnes has an "attachment." David assumes the attachment is to someone new.

Going to the Wickfield house the next day, David relives happy childhood memories. When Agnes walks in, he catches her in his arms for a brotherly hug. Notice how she is described—only her "beautiful serene eyes" and her "angel-face." Their conversation is in tune with his melancholy. He says, as she speaks of Dora and Emily, "I could listen to the sorrowful, distant music, and desire to shrink from nothing it awoke."

---

**NOTE: Dramatic irony**  For once you know more than David does. Earlier, when he foreshadowed Emily's tragedy, he knew what was going to happen and simply hadn't told it yet. Now, however, the older David himself is acting, and he has less perspective on himself. He doesn't seem to understand the meaning behind Agnes' sad, quiet smile. First he tries to get her to confide in him about her lover (he's probably jealous), and she merely blushes and shakes her head, which suggests that David is her "attachment." When he says to her, "Nothing good is difficult to you," she blushes and smiles again, which suggests that her self-sacrifice for David's love has in fact been very painful. But David merely records her expressions, without seeming to understand their meaning.

---

In keeping with this melancholy mood, Mr. Wickfield tells the full story of his own marriage. His wife's father disowned her for marrying Wickfield, and she died of a broken heart soon after Agnes' birth. Though brief, it's one more example of a blighted marriage and an unhealthy parent-child relationship. David's fervent conversation later with Agnes keeps veering close to an admission of love, but only close enough to make Agnes wince, as David harps on her saintliness and what a dear sister she is. Some readers feel that David really loves her for these traits, and therefore they are unconvinced by this relationship. Others feel that David has stronger, more sexual feelings for her but he's not admitting them to himself. She does seem unusually noble, talking about how his writing is important because he can do good through his books. But she also seems suited to his older, changed self. Notice that he praises her for her soft, almost sorrowful spirit. Why does she go on hiding her true feelings? Why is David still hiding his?

As David gets down to work again in the next chapter, he finally mentions how important his writing is to him. He explains why he hasn't talked about it more during the course of his story: because his books should themselves be his proof. Those books have made him so famous that he's getting bags of fan mail, and he enters in partnership with Traddles so that Traddles can be his business manager. Meanwhile, David envies Traddles' happy home, with Sophy copying documents for him and keeping house cleverly on very little money. Traddles gaily describes to David the inexpensive pleasures that make them happy. David remembers Traddles as he was at Salem House and pulls out from his stack of letters one from Mr. Creakle. Their old schoolmaster is now a magistrate, in charge of a prison.

---

**NOTE: Prison satire**  This chapter seems to delay the book's ending, but Dickens' reputation as a political satirist demanded at least one broad satire on an institution, so here it is. Dickens had very strong ideas on prison reform. Although he was a liberal in many respects, he did not believe in treating prisoners kindly, feeling the money could be better spent helping honest people. Therefore, you see the old hypocrite Creakle, who ran his school like a prison, now running a prison like a pleasant school.

It may not be very realistic, but it's fitting that in this prison David meets some old enemies, rounding off their stories. Heep is here, and in his hypocrisy he's convinced the prison officers that he's a model prisoner, repentant and humble. In the very next cell is Littimer, who rivals Heep as a respectable prisoner. These villains are incapable of change. Littimer still tries to make David feel young and inadequate, and Heep, while saying he forgives David, implies that David has been wicked. Heep was arrested, fittingly, for fraud, while Littimer stole from his employer. Even Miss Mowcher is brought back into the plot, when David learns that she nabbed Littimer, probably to settle the score for what he did to Emily.

Despite his fame, David feels melancholy, mostly because of Agnes. He still believes he shouldn't reveal his feelings to Agnes, yet glimmers of hope, dreams of a happy future with her still rise to the surface. His heart is disciplined now, but is this really such a virtue after all? He's so busy restraining his feelings, he can't read Agnes' heart. Ironically, he's upset that she hasn't confided in him about her "attachment," and he worries that she doesn't understand how he feels (meaning how well he's disciplined his heart). When watchful Betsey hints that Agnes may soon marry, David heads for Canterbury in a state of agitation. Note that it's a frozen, wintry day. Since Dickens usually uses weather to set a scene, what kind of scene do you feel is coming?

David confronts Agnes, asking her to share her secret. This conversation is full of emotions trembling just below the surface. Agnes bursts into tears, and hope instinctively leaps into David's heart. For once, Agnes is emotional, while David acts kind and helpful. But because you know he doesn't understand her true feelings, his kind words sound clumsy and stupid. He speaks of his brotherly concern, how he wants to share her burden, how he wouldn't be jealous of another. (Don't these sound like the wrong things to say to someone who's supposed to be in love?) Finally she tells him that her secret is an old one. This is the clue David needs, and he bursts into a confession of his love.

---

**NOTE:** Even as David proposes to Agnes, he speaks of Dora and sees her eyes shining through Agnes'. Perhaps Dickens unconsciously wanted to put a little more of pretty Dora into Agnes so David can love her. Or perhaps Dickens just wanted to show that David is not betraying his love for Dora by marrying Agnes. After they're married, Agnes admits to David that Dora "left" David to Agnes, the night she died. You're reminded of Dora's wisdom, as her blessing on this marriage clears the air of any regrets.

David ties up more threads by dramatizing another scene, ten years later. Mr. Peggotty comes home for a visit from Australia, bearing news of his prosperity and good fortune. His account moves from tragic stories toward comic ones. Emily's spirits have often been low, he says, especially after she learned about Ham and Steerforth's deaths, although hard work and good deeds always got her through. Martha, who is less of a tragic heroine, has fared better and married a farm-laborer. Even Mrs. Gummidge got a proposal of marriage once, though she refused it comically, but otherwise she's been cheerful and helpful the whole time. Mr. Peggotty ends with the most comic character, Mr. Micawber. Even he has worked hard and prospered in Australia and is now a magistrate.

---

**NOTE:**    Though Micawber's fortunes have changed, Dickens assures you that his personality hasn't. You hear Micawber's characteristic speech again in the article Mr. Peggotty shows them from a local paper, describing a public dinner honoring Micawber. As the article goes on, it sounds more and more like Mr. Micawber wrote it. Micawber has also printed a letter to David in the paper, as though he can't resist firing off another wordy letter if he has the chance.

---

The article about the dinner also reveals that Mr. Mell, David's teacher at Salem House, now runs a school in Australia, and Mrs. Micawber's family has gone to Australia, finally approving of Mr. Micawber. One last touching detail ends this chapter:

Mr. Peggotty goes to Yarmouth to pull a tuft of grass from Ham's grave, as he promised to do for Emily.

The final chapter is one last present-tense retrospect, but this time it sounds as though it really is written about the present. David and Agnes are happy, with several children and with David's success still growing. But much of the rest is gently melancholy. You see Betsey, Peggotty, and Mr. Dick grown old, though still using their characteristic props or turns of phrase. Mrs. Steerforth lives on, addled by her stroke; Rosa, withered but fierce as ever, remains tied to her side. Julia Mills has come home from India, where she married a rich man, but she seems disagreeable and unhappy. David describes her social circle with distaste, and Jack Maldon's presence there is a bad sign. David briefly tells you that the Strongs are happy, and Mrs. Markleham no longer interferes. He spends more time depicting Traddles, whose hair still stands on end but who is apparently becoming a success. Traddles uses his money to do good deeds for his wife's family. (Dickens has David describe yet another bad marriage—Sophy's sister "the Beauty" married a shiftless cad.) David's last words are of Agnes, whose face shines like a "Heavenly light" upon him. The book's final image is of Agnes, still pointing upward.

# A STEP BEYOND

## Tests and Answers
### TESTS

### Test 1

1. The Crocodile Book is _____
   A. David's childhood storybook
   B. a legal record at Doctors' Commons
   C. Uriah Heep's secret account book

2. Mr. Mell is a school teacher _____
   I. at Salem House
   II. at Dr. Strong's
   III. in Australia
       A. I only    B. I and II only
       C. I and III only

3. Tommy Traddles is always doodling _____
   A. snakes    B. skeletons
   C. locks and keys

4. Ten-year-old David walks from London to _____
   Dover because
   A. he's following the Micawbers
   B. his money was stolen from him
   C. there's a storm brewing

5. Mr. Wickfield's "one motive" is _____
   A. to send Jack Maldon abroad
   B. to take care of Agnes
   C. to expose Uriah Heep

6. Rosa Dartle's scar was caused by _____
   A. young David biting her

    B. the slip of a surgeon's knife
    C. a hammer Steerforth threw at her

7. Two contrasting ideals of "firmness" are    \_\_\_\_\_
   held by
    A. Mr. Murdstone and Aunt Betsey
    B. Miss Murdstone and Peggotty
    C. Mr. Spenlow and Mr. Jorkins

8. As he gets older, Barkis    \_\_\_\_\_
    A. gets short of breath
    B. becomes a miser
    C. loses his power of speech

9. David's secret courtship of Dora is discov-    \_\_\_\_\_
   ered when
    A. Mr. Mills comes home early
    B. Jip barks from the next room
    C. Miss Murdstone finds his love letters

10. One happy partnership in this book is    \_\_\_\_\_
    A. Omer and Joram
    B. Spenlow and Jorkins
    C. Wickfield and Heep

11. Do you think David is the hero of this book? Why or why not?

12. Are the Micawbers a portrait of a happy family? Defend your answer.

13. Do you think Dickens identifies with David? Support your opinion.

14. Is *David Copperfield* a satirical novel? Discuss specific examples.

# Test 2

1. "Barkis is willing" to      \_\_\_\_\_
   A. marry Clara Peggotty
   B. drive David to Yarmouth
   C. lend David money

2. At Salem House, David wears a sign which   \_\_\_\_\_
   says
   A. "Trotwood Copperfield, Esq."
   B. "Charity orphan"
   C. "Take care of him. He bites."

3. Steerforth reveals Mr. Mell's secret, which   \_\_\_\_\_
   is that
   A. his mother lives in an alms-house
   B. he loves Miss Creakle
   C. he has a wooden leg

4. "The Old Soldier" is a nickname for     \_\_\_\_\_
   A. Miss Murdstone
   B. Annie Strong's mother
   C. Mr. Spenlow

5. The "Memorial" is     \_\_\_\_\_
   A. Mr. Dick's writing about his affairs
   B. the novel David writes about Dora's
      death
   C. the monument Mrs. Steerforth builds
      to her son

6. Aunt Betsey wants David to learn     \_\_\_\_\_
   A. self-control     B. self-respect
   C. self-reliance

7. The character who is always "respectable"   \_\_\_\_\_
   is
   A. Uriah Heep's mother

B. Steerforth's servant Littimer
C. David's landlady Mrs. Crupp

8. Emily's fate is foreshadowed by            _____
   I. Annie Strong
   II. Martha Endell
   III. Rosa Dartle
        A. I and II only      C. I, II, and III
        B. II and III only

9. When David tells Dora he's lost his money,   _____
   she
   A. begins to learn cooking
   B. says Jip must have a chop every day
   C. talks romantically about the Cottage of
      content

10. "In short" is a favorite phrase of            _____
    A. Uriah Heep      B. Miss Mowcher
    C. Mr. Micawber

11. Who is the heroine of this book? Explain.

12. Discuss the role of the servants and waiters in this
    book.

13. How does Dickens "tag" his characters for satiric
    effect?

14. Discuss Dickens' skill as a psychologist.

# ANSWERS

## Test 1

1. A      2. C      3. B      4. B      5. B      6. C
7. A      8. B      9. C      10. A

11. Begin by identifying this question as a reference to

the novel's opening sentence. Then define your use of "hero"—as the main character, the most admirable character, or the subject of the book. You might spend one paragraph discussing how David fulfills (or does not fulfill) each of these "hero" roles. Or, after defining your term, you can devote your answer to proving that David is or is not a hero in one particular sense. If you talk about David as the main character, be sure that you distinguish between his role as the narrator and his role as the protagonist (the main actor in the plot). If you talk about David as the most admirable character, you might want to compare him to other characters to show whether or not David seems more admirable than they are. If you discuss David as the subject of the book, it would be useful to show not only whether the plot revolves around him, but also whether the themes all relate to him.

**12.** First show what makes the Micawbers distinctive in this book—the fact that they are a large family, with both parents, while most of the other families are made up of single children and single parents. Then discuss both sides of the question. What evidence do you have that this is a happy family? What evidence do you have that they are unhappy? Be sure to look at the children as well as the parents, particularly in the later chapters. Finally, state your opinion about them, and defend it. Show how they fit into the values of the book as a whole, especially the theme of families. Explain your own reaction to them; for example, how you feel when you read the passages describing them, or what you imagine it would be like to be part of that family.

**13.** Make some notes before you start writing. First list places in the book where Dickens does not seem to identify with David, such as when David is being blind about

Dora or about Agnes. In the other list, include examples where Dickens does seem to identify with David, such as when he explains about his writing career, when he remembers working in the factory, and when he satirizes political institutions. When you write your answer, try to show both sides before you state your opinion. Also, be careful to distinguish between the older David who is narrating the story and Dickens himself. For example, during David's courtship of Dora, the narrator is consciously poking fun at himself, so Dickens identifies with David the narrator, even if he doesn't totally identify with David the young lover. Remember that Dickens may not be consistent. In some plots, his attitude toward David may be different than in others, as David plays different roles. Try to show the complexity of this question, rather than strain to prove your opinion.

**14.** Begin with a little background on Dickens as a satirist in general, referring to other books and to his life and times, if possible. Then turn to the satire in *David Copperfield*. First outline the topics of satire in this book—fallen women, child labor, education, Doctors' Commons, parliamentary debate, prison reform. Explain how each occurs in the book and the attitude Dickens seems to take toward each one. Describe the different satiric techniques he uses. For example, he may not use a satirical tone when writing about Emily, because melodrama is the most effective way of getting his political message across. Finally, relate the satire to the book as a whole. Are these satiric passages central to the book? Is the novel's overall tone satiric? Don't be afraid to base your answer on your own feelings. Show which elements you feel are strongest or most believable, even if they may not be Dickens' main concerns.

## Test 2

1. A    2. C    3. A    4. B    5. A    6. C
7. B    8. C    9. B    10. C

**11.** Set up the reason for this question by explaining that Dickens himself regarded Agnes, as opposed to Dora, as the "real heroine." You may want to discuss your definition of "heroine"—the hero's mate, the most admirable woman character, or the book's main female interest. Compare David's relationships with Dora and Agnes and discuss how each one seems to relate to the book's themes. Then state which one you feel to be the heroine. Support your choice by showing how that character fits into the book's themes and values. You may also be subjective—talk about which character is more effective and has more impact upon your imagination. Refer to specific passages, however. You may even want to propose another character as the novel's heroine, such as Betsey or Emily. If you do this, keep your discussion of Dora and Agnes brief and announce early that you think neither one is the heroine. Then show how your heroine fits one or all of the roles of a heroine better.

**12.** Try to work through the book chronologically, discussing various incidents where David deals with servants or waiters. These will range from the occasional waiter at an inn (as in Chapters V and LIX) to David's household servants (beginning with Mrs. Crupp and concluding with the page who gets arrested). Discuss what you learn about David from the way he handles hired help. You may then want to look at how other characters deal with their servants: Clara Copperfield with Peggotty, the Micawbers with the Orfling, or the Steerforths with Littimer. Discuss how these relationships illustrate the novel's themes, especially regarding discipline and families. If you think the role of servants expresses Dickens' view of society in some way, explain.

**13.** Discuss various methods Dickens uses to signal his characters' personality traits with quick identifying "tags." You may want to list some examples in each of these categories: stock phrases (Barkis, Mr. Micawber, Mr. Wickfield, Uriah Heep), compulsive gestures (Miss Murdstone, Tommy Traddles, Uriah Heep), or a dominant adjective (Mr. Murdstone, Uriah Heep, Littimer). Also consider Dickens' brilliant use of names. Write about several different names, such as Murdstone, Gummidge, Steerforth, Traddles, Creakle, Heep, Dartle, or Spenlow. For each one, describe the image it creates in your mind, and relate it to the personality of that character. Also discuss the number of different names David answers to—Mas'r Davy, Trotwood, Daisy, Doady—and discuss how these names reflect his changing personality.

**14.** Although psychology had not yet become a science in Dickens' time, he intuitively understood many of its principles. Discuss specific examples from the book where Dickens probes the workings of the human mind. In the earlier chapters, you may want to concentrate on his acute insights into child psychology. For his adult psychology, look at the unbalanced personalities, like Uriah Heep and Rosa Dartle, and more ordinary people's little neuroses, such as Miss Murdstone's repressed love for her brother or the gruff front Betsey presents to the world. You may also want to look at Dickens' descriptions of disordered states of mind, such as drunkenness, infatuation, and dreams.

# Term Paper Ideas and other Topics for Writing

## Themes

**1.** Discuss David's development as a writer, and how it works as a theme of the novel.

**2.** Look at the different "homes" David has. What is each lacking? What is David searching for in a home?

**3.** Compare David's love for Dora to his love for Agnes. Which do you think Dickens prefers? Which do you prefer? Why?

**4.** Choose which marriage in the book you think is the best, and which is the worst. Compare them.

**5.** Discuss at least three of the single parents in the novel and examine their relationships to their children.

**6.** Relate the major themes of this novel to events in Dickens' life.

## Characters

**1.** Compare David to Tommy Traddles. What does this comparison teach you about David?

**2.** Is Uriah Heep a realistic character or a caricature? Define your terms and defend your opinion.

**3.** Do you think Micawber's success in Australia is believable? Why or why not?

**4.** Discuss Clara Copperfield from two angles: as David sees her and as Dickens sees her.

**5.** Discuss James Steerforth from two angles: as David sees him with his head and as David sees him with his heart.

**6.** Do you think Dickens created believable women? Defend your answer by discussing at least three female characters from *David Copperfield*. Compare them to female characters from other Dickens novels, if you can.

**7.** Choose one of these minor characters and discuss his or her role in the novel: Dr. Chillip, Barkis, Mrs. Gummidge, Mr. Omer, Mrs. Markleham, Mrs. Crupp, Mr. Jorkins, Sophy.

## Techniques
**1.** Discuss the image of drowning.

**2.** Analyze the speech of one of these characters: Mr. Micawber, Uriah Heep, Rosa Dartle, Miss Mowcher. Discuss how speech patterns define the character's personality, referring to specific passages.

**3.** Discuss Dickens' use of cinematic techniques, with reference to specific scenes.

**4.** Compare the climactic scenes of each of these plots: Emily/Ham/Steerforth, Wickfield/Heep, David/Dora, David/Agnes.

## Background
**1.** Was David's experience in the wine warehouse typical for those times? Research the history of child labor and its reform in England.

**2.** Find the different settings of *David Copperfield* on a map of England. How far apart were they, and what would they have looked like in the early nineteenth century? How would railroads change this English landscape?

**3.** What were the different courts in nineteenth-century England, including Doctor's Commons? What different kinds of lawyers were there? How would a firm like Wickfield & Heep differ from Spenlow & Jorkins?

# Further Reading
## CRITICAL WORKS

### Biographies

Forster, John. *The Life of Charles Dickens*. 2 vols. London: S. M. Dent & Sons, 1872–1874.

Johnson, Edgar. *Charles Dickens, His Tragedy and Triumph*. 2 vols. New York: Simon & Schuster, 1952.

Wilson, Angus. *The World of Charles Dickens*. New York: Viking Press, 1970.

### General Criticism

Carey, John. *The Violent Effigy*. London: Faber & Faber, 1973. U.S. title: *Here Comes Dickens*. New York: Schocken Books, 1974.

Chesterton, G. K. *Charles Dickens*. New York: Schocken Books, 1965.

Collins, Philip. *Charles Dickens: David Copperfield*. London: Edward Arnold, Ltd., 1977.

Fielding, K. J. *Charles Dickens: A Critical Introduction*. New York: Longman, 1958.

Ford, George H., and Lauriat Lane, eds. *The Dickens Critics*. Ithaca, New York: Cornell University Press, 1961.

Gissing, George. *Dickens, A Critical Study*. New York: Haskell House, repr 1965.

Gross, John, and Gabriel Pearson, eds. *Dickens and the Twentieth Century*. London: Routledge & Kegan Paul, 1962.

Hobsbaum, Philip. *A Reader's Guide to Charles Dickens*. London: Thames & Hudson, Ltd., 1972.

House, Humphrey. *The Dickens World*. London: Oxford University Press, 1941.

Leavis, F. R. & Q. D. *Dickens the Novelist*. New York: Pantheon Books, 1970.

Maurois, André. *Dickens*. Translated by Hamish Miles. New York: J. Lane, 1934.

Monod, Sylvere. *Dickens the Novelist*. Norman, Oklahoma: University of Oklahoma Press, 1968.

Price, Martin, ed. *Dickens: A Collection of Critical Essays*. Englewood Cliffs, New Jersey: Prentice-Hall, 1967.

Wilson, Edmund. *The Wound and the Bow*. Boston: Houghton Mifflin, 1947.

Zabel, Morton Dauwen. *Craft and Character*. New York: Viking Press, 1957.

# AUTHOR'S OTHER WORKS

*Sketches by Boz*, 1834–36
*Pickwick Papers*, 1836–37
*Oliver Twist*, 1837
*Nicholas Nickleby*, 1838–39
*The Old Curiosity Shop*, 1840–41
*Barnaby Rudge*, 1841
*Martin Chuzzlewit*, 1843–44
*A Christmas Carol*, 1843
*Dombey and Son*, 1846–48
*Bleak House*, 1852–53
*Hard Times*, 1854
*Little Dorrit*, 1855–57
*A Tale of Two Cities*, 1859
*Great Expectations*, 1860–61
*Our Mutual Friend*, 1864–65
*The Mystery of Edwin Drood*, 1870

# Glossary

**Adelphi**   A large complex of apartments in London.

**Book of Martyrs**   A popular book written in Latin by John Foxe, which first appeared in English in 1563.

**Charing Cross**   An ancient stone cross that marked a coach terminus for arrivals to London.

**Doctors' Commons**   A variety of courts sharing the same buildings and the same specialist lawyers (their offices were also part of the commons). It became part of the Probate Court in 1857.

**Don Quixote**   A Spanish novel by Miguel de Cervantes.

**Enfield's Speaker**   A book published in 1832 by W. J. Enfield, *The Speaker: Selections from the Best English Writers.*

**gaiters**   A cloth or leather leg-covering.

**father-in-law**   Stepfather.

**Gil Blas**   A French novel by Le Sage.

**Humphrey Clinker**   A novel by Tobias Smollett.

**Inner Temple**   One of the Inns of Court, a neighborhood of lawyers' lodgings and offices packed around quiet courtyards.

**Lincoln's Inns Fields**   Near the Inns of Court, a small park surrounded by townhouses and offices.

**Peregrine Pickle**   A novel by Tobias Smollett.

**Robinson Crusoe**   A novel by Daniel Defoe.

**Roderick Random**   A novel by Tobias Smollett.

**Tidd's Practice**   A standard legal textbook by William Tidd, *Practice of the Court of King's Bench*, published between 1790 and 1794.

**Tom Jones**   A novel by Henry Fielding.

**Tower**   The Tower of London, an ancient Norman castle in London.

**The Vicar of Wakefield**   A novel by Oliver Goldsmith.

# The Critics

Dickens . . . was . . . the greatest dramatic writer that the English had had since Shakespeare, and he created the largest and most varied world.

> Edmund Wilson, *The Wound and the Bow*, 1947.

Dickens's fictional world is populous but tidy—a world with abundant poetic justice, problems solved, and no loose ends.

> Philip Collins, *Charles Dickens: David Copperfield*, 1977.

[Dickens'] books are full of baffled villains stalking out or cowardly bullies kicked downstairs. But the villains and the cowards are such delightful people that the reader always hopes the villain will put his head through a side window and make a last remark; or that the bully will say one more thing, even from the bottom of the stairs.

> G. K. Chesterton, *Charles Dickens*, 1906.

That Dickens was a great genius and is permanently among the classics is certain. But the genius was that of a great entertainer, and he had for the most part no profounder responsibility as a creative artist than this description suggests.

> F. R. Leavis, *The Great Tradition*, 1950.

Like the Victorian age itself, with its surface of exuberant confidence . . . and its undersurface of uncertainty, the appearance of Dickens's happy position was a deceptive and incomplete indication of his state of mind.

> George Ford, introduction to *David Copperfield*, 1958.

When people say Dickens exaggerates, it seems to me they can have no eyes and no ears. They probably have only notions of what things and people are; they accept them conventionally, at their diplomatic value.

> George Santayana, "Dickens," in
> *The Dial*, 1921.

Dickens' London may be different from actual London, but it is just as real, its streets are of firm brick, its inhabitants genuine flesh and blood . . . . It does not matter that Dickens' world is not lifelike: it is alive.

> David Cecil, *Early Victorian
> Novelists*, 1934.

The outstanding, unmistakeable mark of Dickens' writing is the unnecessary detail . . . . He is all fragments, all detail—rotten architecture, but wonderful gargoyles.

> George Orwell, "Charles
> Dickens," 1940.

Dickens is always great on the subject of childhood—that sunny time, as it is conventionally called, but which, as Dickens represents it, and as we recollect it, is somewhat showery withal.

> Unsigned review, *Fraser's
> Magazine*, 1850.

When [Dickens] suggests, as he does repeatedly, that *Copperfield* is really about 'the mistaken impulse of an undisciplined heart,' we don't believe him; this is a clear case of 'Never trust the artist, trust the tale'—the tale being not an affair of Theme, of subjects, at all.

> John Jones, "David Copperfield,"
> in *Dickens and the Twentieth
> Century*, 1962.